D1607571

How Does 3D Printing Work?

IAN CHOW-MILLER

HERRICK DISTRICT LIBRARY
300 S. River Avenue
Holland, MI 49423

MAR 20 2018

Cavendish
Square
New York

Published in 2018 by Cavendish Square Publishing, LLC
243 5th Avenue, Suite 136, New York, NY 10016

Copyright © 2018 by Cavendish Square Publishing, LLC

First Edition

No part of this publication may be reproduced, stored in a retrieval system, or transmitted in any form or by any means—electronic, mechanical, photocopying, recording, or otherwise—without the prior permission of the copyright owner. Request for permission should be addressed to Permissions, Cavendish Square Publishing, 243 5th Avenue, Suite 136, New York, NY 10016. Tel (877) 980-4450; fax (877) 980-4454.

Website: cavendishsq.com

This publication represents the opinions and views of the author based on his or her personal experience, knowledge, and research. The information in this book serves as a general guide only. The author and publisher have used their best efforts in preparing this book and disclaim liability rising directly or indirectly from the use and application of this book.

All websites were available and accurate when this book was sent to press.

Library of Congress Cataloging-in-Publication Data

Names: Chow-Miller, Ian, author.
Title: How does 3D printing work? / Ian Chow-Miller.
Description: New York : Cavendish Square Publishing, 2018. | Series:
Project learning with 3D printing | Includes index.
Identifiers: LCCN 2017029857 (print) | LCCN 2017031023 (ebook) |
ISBN 9781502631572 (E-book) | ISBN 9781502631565 (library bound) | ISBN 9781502634252 (pbk.)
Subjects: LCSH: Three-dimensional printing--Juvenile literature.
Classification: LCC TS171.95 (ebook) | LCC TS171.95 .C49 2018 (print) | DDC 621.9/88--dc23
LC record available at https://lccn.loc.gov/2017029857

Editorial Director: David McNamara
Editor: Fletcher Doyle
Copy Editor: Nathan Heidelberger
Associate Art Director: Amy Greenan
Designer: Alan Sliwinski
Production Coordinator: Karol Szymczuk
Photo Research: J8 Media

The photographs in this book are used by permission and through the courtesy of: Cover David Stock/Alamy Stock Photo; p. 4 Mike Calvo/National Geographic Magazines/ Getty Images; p. 8, 18, 21, 22, 23, 24, 31, 38, 40, 42, 43, 56, 57, 62, 66, 69, 74, 76, 78, 82, 83, 87, 88, 91, 93, 95, 99, 102, 104, 105, 107, 110, 113, 115 Ian Chow Miller; p. 26 Erik Tham/ Corbis/Getty Images; p. 48 Keon Boozarjomehri; p. 72 asharkyu/Shutterstock.com.

Printed in the United States of America

CONTENTS

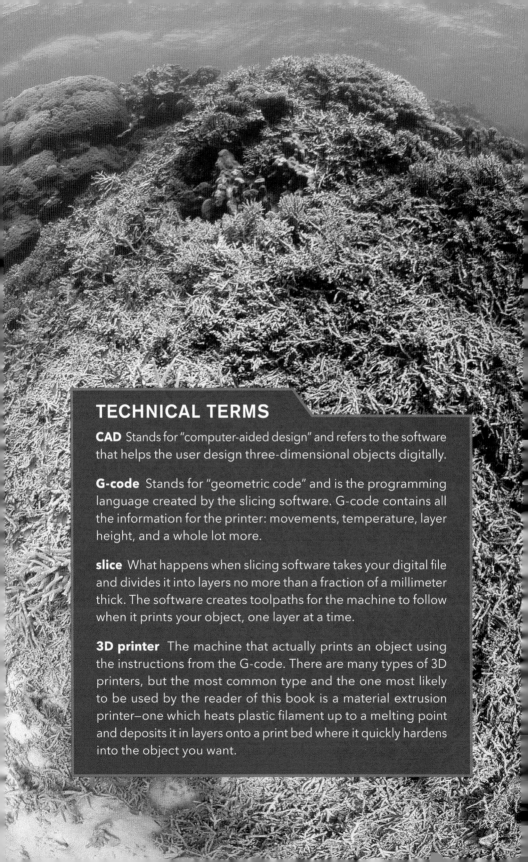

TECHNICAL TERMS

CAD Stands for "computer-aided design" and refers to the software that helps the user design three-dimensional objects digitally.

G-code Stands for "geometric code" and is the programming language created by the slicing software. G-code contains all the information for the printer: movements, temperature, layer height, and a whole lot more.

slice What happens when slicing software takes your digital file and divides it into layers no more than a fraction of a millimeter thick. The software creates toolpaths for the machine to follow when it prints your object, one layer at a time.

3D printer The machine that actually prints an object using the instructions from the G-code. There are many types of 3D printers, but the most common type and the one most likely to be used by the reader of this book is a material extrusion printer—one which heats plastic filament up to a melting point and deposits it in layers onto a print bed where it quickly hardens into the object you want.

CHAPTER ONE

Introduction to 3D Printing

F OR MANY YEARS, THE SCIENTIFIC COMMUNITY HAS BEEN sounding the alarm about the decline of coral reef systems around the world. These fragile ecosystems are massive and perform many important functions: they protect coastlines from harmful erosion, contain some of the most diverse ecosystems on the planet, and simultaneously provide habitat for a multitude of marine life. The collapse of coral reefs would of course take away all these benefits, and unfortunately that is what has been happening recently. Coral reefs have been dying due to a phenomenon known as "bleaching."

Opposite: Large areas of the Great Barrier Reef off the coast of Australia have undergone bleaching. Efforts are under way in some places to 3D print structures for new coral reefs.

Bleaching is a process whereby algae that live in the reefs and that the coral feeds on leave in large numbers due to warmer than normal waters. As climate change has been heating up oceans worldwide, the process has accelerated, and scientists are becoming more and more worried. According to *National Geographic*, the Great Barrier Reef in Australia (the largest reef in the world) lost a fourth of its coral in 2016 due to bleaching and was due to suffer another catastrophic loss in 2017. Simply put, we need to replace the coral reefs around the world before it's too late.

One of the things being attempted is the production of artificial reefs. Artificial reefs are nothing new. You've most likely seen movies of sunken ships with fish swimming in and out of them. Scientists have tried a variety of other objects to create reefs, such as cement blocks, old cars, construction debris, etc. None of these objects works perfectly. While fish and other marine life can use some of the object as a habitat, the object doesn't have the right structure: the classic curves of coral reefs with the thousands of holes that fish can swim through and be protected in. So scientists are turning to another solution: **3D printing** coral reefs.

By 3D printing artificial reefs, their exact structure can be replicated. The right density, proper curves, the exact height, the right amount of holes, even the proper color can be 3D printed. I think color might be more aimed at pleasing tourists than fish, but it can still be done. Printed coral reefs have been placed in most of the major oceans and bodies of water where coral reefs have suffered damage. With the right materials, coral polyps attach themselves to the structure and form new coral reefs, hopefully saving the fragile ecosystems. Amazing advances like this would not have been possible just a quarter century ago.

From Small Beginnings

3D printing has come a long way in its relatively short, approximately twenty-five-year history. The things that can be done with 3D printing are amazing—and in the case of activities like remaking the dying coral reefs around the world, revolutionary. Doctors are 3D printing casts and bones and are even attempting to 3D print organs. Companies are using large **3D printers** to print houses in record time and at fractions of the cost of building the usual way. Car manufacturers are printing parts for their automobiles. The list goes on and on. 3D printing has taken the world by storm recently, and it is expanding in many ways, perhaps including some ways that haven't been revealed.

While the next big thing with 3D printing may be just around the corner, one of the great advances has been in bringing down the cost and availability of printers to make them available to users like you and me. I received my first 3D printer—it was called a RapMan for "Rapid Manufacturing"—from my boss a few years ago, and it was from a company that has since gone out of business.

The author's two classroom 3D printers are a Rostock Max V2 (*left*) and a Dremel 3D20 Idea Builder (*right*).

I built it, installed firmware to run it, and then printed one of the stock prints built into the firmware: a gargoyle pencil topper. And then it broke. A part had failed, and with a little internet research I learned that the part (a gear in the **extruder**, which we'll get to later) failed often on this particular printer. Apparently a lot of people knew this and were printing replacement parts to improve their printer as soon as they got one. So it went like this: buy the printer, print a part to improve the printer, swap out the new part for the old, and the printer doesn't fail. This was great if you were a hobbyist and in the know and active in online 3D printing forums. However, that was not the case for me, nor was it reasonable to expect a middle school robotics teacher to know this.

I relay the above tale because it took place in 2013–four years before this book was written. It was 2013, and I had a 3D printer in my classroom that was basically useless to me. In the summer of 2015, I received and built my second 3D printer, a Rostock Max V2 desktop 3D printer from the company SeeMeCNC. This was an excellent printer, and even though it took me a while to build (eighteen hours over three days), I was able to print the nose cones for my students' rockets one semester. At some point, however, I damaged the heat resistor, which is about the width of a human hair, and it took me days to get a replacement part and then many hours rebuilding the printer to get it working again.

Fast forward to September 2016. I received a Dremel 3D20 Idea Builder. This one came in a box and took two of my eighth-grade students one period to set up. By the next period, they had printed a cute little bear. That machine has worked since, and I have used it far more than the previous two. My point here is that while the future of 3D printing may be an artificial kidney for a big biomedical firm, the future for people like me is printers that are easier to assemble, are more affordable, and work better. It's these types of printers that are going to be the focus of this book.

Fundamentals

So what exactly is 3D printing? It is a process of making items using what is called **additive manufacturing**.

Additive manufacturing is exactly what it sounds like; you make something by adding material to it. In the case of 3D printing, you are adding each layer of material at fractions of a millimeter at a time. Additive manufacturing is, perhaps obviously, the opposite of **subtractive manufacturing**. Subtractive manufacturing has been around a lot longer than additive. When you carve a stick into a sharp spear, you are technically using subtractive manufacturing. You are subtracting material as you carve. Machines like a **CNC mill** use subtractive manufacturing by operating a drill point to cut away material from a solid block in order to create a shape or item.

There are three main steps to 3D printing any object. The first is to create a digital file. This can be accomplished in a few ways. You can use **CAD** (computer-aided design) software to create a 3D image of the object. You can also use a scanner that takes a three-dimensional picture of an object. This is how bobbleheads with different people's faces are printed. You can also find an immense array of digital files already hosted on the internet for you to print. Chapter 2 will focus on creating or obtaining a digital file for 3D printing. Let's take a look at step two.

The second step is **slicing** the file. Once you have your three-dimensional digital image, you need to import that image into a slicing program. What the slicing program does is take that image and slice it into layers. Depending on the program, the printer, and your personal choice, the layers can be anywhere from about 0.05 millimeters thick to 2 millimeters thick (0.002 to 0.08 inches). Slicing software usually works with many different printers as long as they are all of the same type (more on printer types later). For example, Autodesk Print Studio, which I use often, connects to printers by Dremel, Printrbot, MakerBot, and a few others. Some slicing software is specific to an individual printer; for example the Dremel 3D Idea Builder software works with Dremel printers only.

3D PRINTING TIP

A **raft** is a common option in slicing software that can save your print. A raft is a thin layer of plastic printed in a loose weave (not solid), designed to separate easily both from the **print bed** and the object. The purpose of the raft is to prevent the object from sticking to the print bed.

Slicing software doesn't only cut up your digital image into layers; it can do a lot more. Depending on the sophistication of the software, it can also adjust the temperature of different parts of your printer (**nozzle** of the extruder and print bed), **scale** the size of your print, adjust the layer thickness, change the fill type and percentage, provide **supports**, add rafts, control speed, and a host of other even more esoteric options. If terms like "fill," "raft," "support" and others sound bewildering to you, they will be discussed in detail in chapter 3. Chapter 3 will look at several different slicing programs and discuss their pros and cons. When your slicing software is done processing your digital image, it will **export G-code** and send that to your printer.

G-code

"Ain't nuthin' but a G-code thang baby," is a horrible play on words for a middle-aged teacher like myself to use. Not only have you dated yourself because Dr. Dre and Snoop Dogg rapped the original lyrics over fifteen years ago, but any overt attempt by a forty-six-year-old teacher to make himself look cool is probably going to end in failure. However, there is a lot of truth to the phrase. Specifically, there is a lot of truth to saying that 3D printing isn't much more than a fancy machine utilizing what we call G-code. G-code is the set of instructions underpinning everything a 3D printer does. As a matter of fact, G-code is pretty much what runs most manufacturing machines like laser cutters, plasma cutters, CNC (computer numerical control) mills, and of course 3D printers.

G-code stands for "geometric code," and it is a series of recognized commands that can be sent to any

3D PRINTING TIP

One of the most useful things slicing software can do for you is to provide supports. Supports will hold up any overhanging section of a printed object. Your software can determine where supports are needed and how many to create, and you can choose the type of supports you want for your print.

printer. Each code is associated with a specific command. For example, the most utilized G-code is G01, which essentially means to move in a straight line. You will see it written like this:

G01 X24 Y17 F500 E0.1

This command tells the nozzle on the printer to move in a straight line from the current position to the coordinates X24 and Y17. The F command indicates the feed rate or speed, and the E command is the extrusion rate. If you look at the G-code for any 3D print, there will be hundreds or even thousands of lines. The majority of them will be G01 commands, as moving the print nozzle is the most common action a 3D printer will take.

There will also be many one-time commands. For example, G0 followed by x and y coordinates will move the nozzle to a specific point using rapid motion. This is usually used at the beginning of a program to send the nozzle to a starting point; this is why there is no feed rate or extrusion rate associated with G0. There are many other common G-code commands. For example, G28 sends the print nozzle to a home position, while G20 sets units to inches and G21 sets units to millimeters. The feed rate F from the earlier G01 command depends on what the units are set to. In the example above, if G20 was included in the code, then the feed rate would be 500 inches per minute, as the feed rate for 3D printers is always inches or millimeters per minute.

When we look at slicing software in chapter 3, we will examine a portion of exported G-code in detail. While you can print files directly from a slicing program without ever looking at the G-code, it is helpful to know and understand it. And if you seriously get into 3D printing, learning G-code is an essential tool. It lets you catch errors and make minute adjustments to your print file.

The first two steps, the creation of digital CAD files and the slicing of such a file into thousands of layers, would be academic exercises at best without the subject of this book, 3D printers. As we've mentioned, 3D printers are machines that build an item using additive manufacturing. There are many different types and categories of these printers, which we'll examine below.

Additive Manufacturing

In 2009, the American Society for Testing and Materials (https://www.astm.org) formed a working group, ASTM F42, to help standardize and categorize the different types of additive manufacturing processes. While the layman may think of 3D printing as a machine that puts layers of melted plastic on top of each other, there are actually many different categories of additive manufacturing. The ASTM developed seven categories of additive manufacturing. As this is the introductory book in this series, we will spend the majority of this book examining what is the most common type for schools and hobbyists—**material extrusion**. I do, however, want to briefly summarize the other six.

VAT Photopolymerization

A large vat of liquid polymer resin is hardened by repeated passes of ultraviolet light. The vat is moved downward by the lowering of a platform, and the light is moved across the x **axis** (side to side) and y axis (front to back) by a motor. Each layer of the resin hardens when it comes into contact with the ultraviolet light. At the end, the vat is emptied, and the nonhardened liquid pours out while what remains is your object.

Material Jetting

Material is dropped onto a build platform in the form of droplets of liquid plastic. The material is left to harden after each layer is dropped, then the next layer is added.

Binder Jetting

In binder jetting, a layer of powder is placed on the build platform, followed by a layer of some type of binding liquid in the formation of the desired object. Another layer of powder is added, which binds to the liquid binder and hardens. This process is repeated until the object itself is complete.

Powder Bed Fusion

This process is similar to binder jetting but instead of liquid binding to a powder, a laser is used to bind powder material together. In order to take place, this method requires a vacuum in which to operate but can be used to fuse metals and alloys, again one layer at a time.

Sheet Lamination

I was surprised to learn about this method, as it is an additive process that is mixed with a subtractive process. Thin layers (sheets) of metal are layered on top of each other and then welded using an ultrasonic welding technique. After the required thickness is achieved, the remaining material can be cut away (subtractive). Alternately, a laser or knife can be used to cut the material to the desired shape first.

Directed Energy Deposition

This method is one of the most complex and is used to fix objects rather than make new ones. A nozzle is attached to a four- or five-axis arm, which moves around a fixed object and deposits powder or wire material that is melted, by a laser or other means. It is then allowed to harden before the next layer is added.

If the above methods sound complex or even confusing, I found them that way myself. Certainly they are not the sorts of methods or type of printers I could afford or be allowed to operate in my middle school classroom. They usually don't let me operate lasers inside of a vacuum or melt and fuse metal using electrons or ultrasonic beams. Maybe in a few years. But one thing they all have in common in their descriptions is that they build something using layers, thus they are types of additive manufacturing. The final type of additive manufacturing is the one that the rest of this book will concentrate on: material extrusion.

Extrusion

Material extrusion is a process in which material, usually plastic, is fed through a nozzle at a really high temperature and pushed out onto a build platform. This is the basic way material extrusion works, but there are many different variations. In some cases, the nozzle is moved along an x and y axis while the platform itself lowers along the z axis. Other methods have the nozzle moving up and down on the z axis while the platform is what moves along the x and y. And there are other combinations with the platform moving along the z and either x or y, with the print nozzle moving along whatever axis is left out. Finally, there are **delta printers** like the Rostock Max printers that have a fixed print bed and three arms that attach to the print nozzle and move up and down all at the same time.

Printers that use material extrusion are the most common type found in schools and people's homes. They can be relatively small and easy to use. These are often referred to as **desktop printers** for obvious reasons, and the rest of this book will cover the use of these printers and associated software in detail. But first let's take a

The MakerBot Replicator is a material extrusion 3D printer that can fit on your desktop.

look at the history of 3D printing and how we got to the place in 2017 where for under $1,000 I can purchase a printer, take it home, and start making objects within minutes.

History

The history of 3D printing is relatively short, and we really are just in its beginning phases. It is too early to tell where it is going, but we're close enough to the start that we can examine the beginning pretty accurately. While many people had been toying with what was called "rapid prototyping" technology in the early 1980s, the first patent for a **stereolithography** apparatus was issued to Charles Hull in 1983. Stereolithography refers to the process of turning liquid plastic into a solid object using ultraviolet (UV) light. The apparatus was the machine that followed the G-code created by sending 3D digital files into slicing software. Using his patent, he cofounded a company, 3D Systems Corporation, and built one of the first 3D printers. His company is one of the largest organizations in the 3D printing business today.

3D Systems sold its first printer in 1987, and around this time many other companies were coming on board with their own machines. Next came two events that would shape the industry for the future. First, in 1989, Scott Crump, a cofounder of Stratasys Inc., filed a patent for **fused deposition modeling (FDM)**. This process is very similar to the extrusion modeling covered earlier in this chapter and formed the basis for most of the inexpensive desktop models we have today. However, as FDM was patented and copyrighted, it was unavailable for use outside of Stratasys.

Around the same time, the **RepRap** community (http://www.reprap.org) was born, and the term **fused filament fabrication (FFF)** was coined. The RepRap community is an organization dedicated to open-source 3D printing technology. It encourages people to build their own 3D printers and specifically build 3D printers that can build their own parts (so called self-replicators). They are dedicated to sharing their own files, software, plans, and ideas, and to keeping everything open source. The term FFF refers to basically the same process as FDM, but FFF was not copyrighted and was freely available to use.

With advances in technology and an open-source community dedicated to bringing 3D printing to the masses, it was only a matter of time before competition made printers more readily available, cheaper, and better. The printer that I referred to at the beginning of this chapter, the RapMan from BitsFromBytes, was one of the first machines produced using the open-source information available from the RepRap project.

While in 2007 the first "home use" printers cost around $10,000, the RapMan cost close to $2,000. In September of 2016, my school district purchased my Dremel 3D20 Idea Builder for $900. There are other similar products out there like the MakerBot Replicator–which was made by a group that broke off from the RepRap project–the LulzBot, the FlashForge Finder, the Ultimaker, and many more, with new ones coming onto the market almost monthly. These all retail for between $500 and $2,500 each, with the main differences being print speed, print volume, and print detail.

Accurately predicting the future is a tricky business. I'm not sure, and nobody totally is, where 3D printing will go next. I'm not a scientist or futurist, and I think it would be disingenuous to try to guess what the next big thing will be. However, if current trends persist, we will most likely continue to see a decline in price and an improvement in quality of 3D printers at the home/school/hobby use level.

There are two things I want to look at before we push on to the chapters examining CAD, slicing programs, and printers themselves. The first has to do with some of the amazing things I have seen done with 3D printers, including LEGO 3D printers. Yes, you read that correctly: 3D printers made out of LEGO EV3 robotics kits and a few extra parts.

Marc-André Bazergui built the first LEGO EV3 printer I ever came across. I saw it at the Tufts University LEGO Engineering Symposium in June 2016. I could hardly believe what I was seeing at first, but right in front of my eyes a printer made out of LEGO was printing a little Christmas tree–like object. It was more of an exploration of what could be accomplished with a 3D printer than any specific object, but it was still really cool.

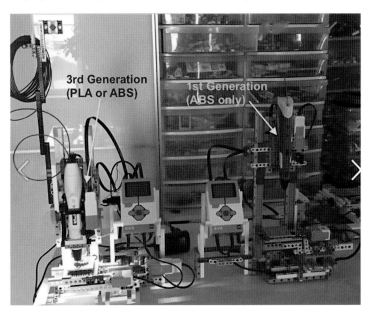

These two LEGO 3D printers were built by Marc-André Bazergui.

The second LEGO 3D printer I saw was also made using an EV3 programmable brick, and while this one may not have been any better (I didn't do a comparative test), it was way more spectacular in that it was built by the Seshan brothers, who happen to be twelve and fourteen years old. The Seshan brothers are two boys from Pittsburgh who have gone way beyond with the work they do in LEGO robotics. They run an outstanding website, http://www.ev3lessons.com, which teaches robotics in a really easy to understand and follow manner. They also have another web page, http://www.beyondtheinstructions.com/projects, that showcases all the work they do with robotics, including their 3D printer.

Both of the printers made by Bazergui and the Seshan brothers run by reading G-code and then moving appropriately. In the printer in the photo below, the nozzle moves up and down on the z axis while the print

The Seshan brothers show off their 3D printer (*middle*) and other inventions.

LENDING A HELPING HAND

The Cyborg Beast—a 3D-printed hand by Jorge Zuniga from Enabling the Future

Jose Delgado Jr. was born without a left hand. Early in his life, he used a cheap prosthesis. He later got a myoelectric prosthesis that used a sensor that sent a signal to move his artificial fingers when he flexed his left arm. This prosthesis cost $42,000, most of which was not covered by insurance. Delgado found an organization called Enabling the Future (http://enablingthefuture.org) on the internet. Enabling the Future is a community of people dedicated to 3D printing arms and hands for free for people in need around the world.

Through Enabling the Future, Delgado contacted Jeremy Simon, who helped him find and print a replacement hand. The hand was based on a design created by Jorge Zuniga called the Cyborg Beast (find it at https://www.thingiverse.com). Simon adapted Zuniga's design to fit Delgado. The cost of materials was $50. In a story published by 3duniverse.org, Delgado says, "When I first put it on [I thought], 'Wow, I can bend all five fingers.'" The prosthesis helps Delgado grip objects—he works in a warehouse moving boxes.

bed moves along the x and y axes. This is different from most material extrusion printers; usually the platform moves up and down on the z axis, not the print nozzle.

Both LEGO printers were made possible by using a new product that can loosely be described as a 3D pen. These pens are roughly the size of magic markers and function by taking in **filament** at the top (the same filament 3D printers use), heating that filament, and then extruding it out the bottom the same way a much fancier extruder works on any 3D printer.

By building their printers using these pens, the inventors are able to get around the need to heat their LEGO pieces to the point at which they might melt. You

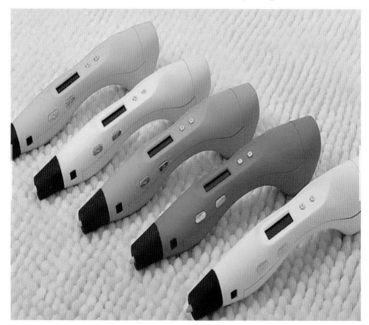

3D pens have allowed students to build 3D printers out of LEGO pieces without melting the LEGO blocks themselves due to exposure to extreme heat.

can also see that they used a much stronger material for their print bed as opposed to using a LEGO plate that might melt.

Even in 2013, when I received my first printer, I would have been shocked to hear that someday soon I would be witnessing one made out of LEGO. As astounding as these are and as impressive as it is to see one made by young teenagers, the true promise of 3D printers in my eyes is in what they can do to make the world a better place.

The futurist Jeremy Rifkin wrote in *The Zero Marginal Cost Society: The Internet of Things, the Collaborative Commons, and the Eclipse of Capitalism*: "The democratization of manufacturing means that anyone and eventually everyone can access the means of production, making the question of who should own and control the means of production irrelevant."

In chapter 5, I am going to take you step by step through the process of designing and printing a **fidget spinner**–those ever-popular toys of the moment. And while my students are loving the ability to design their own spinners, it is stories like the ones above that make me most hopeful about the promise of 3D printing for the future.

TECHNICAL TERMS

direct modeling A newer type of CAD software that allows you to directly create objects by choosing premade shapes and manipulating their shape and size by dragging corners and making other movements with your mouse.

extrude A common CAD term in parametric modeling; to extrude means to add a third dimension to a sketched, closed figure by pulling or pushing it along a third axis.

parametric modeling A type of CAD software where you design the object from scratch, adding geometric constraints and dimensions to give it exact shape and size. Parametric models have a history you can access so you can go back to earlier versions of the model and change dimensions or constraints to change the final version.

shell Another common CAD term which means to cut out a section inside a digital object. For example if you have a cube that is 3 × 3 × 3 inches, and you draw a 2.9-inch square on one face, by "shelling" you can hollow out the cube so that the sides are only 0.05 inches thick all around.

CHAPTER TWO

Creating Your Own Digital File

THE WORLD IS FULL OF CREATIVE PEOPLE WHO CAN MAKE and design amazing things. I am not one of those people. I never have been and probably never will be. My wife is an art teacher, and I've always been envious of what she is capable of when it comes to almost any creative medium. I'm quite a believer that anyone's skills can be improved through learning and practice, but I also have a strong belief in talent. Some people have artistic talent, some don't. You know where I fall in that dichotomy. Luckily, there are tools that can help me out.

Computer-aided design (CAD) tools have come a long way in their nearly fifty-year history. Not only have

Opposite: An object designed using CAD software shows the geometric shapes that will comprise the item.

they gotten better at what they do, they have become easier to use. In recent years, many of them have been aimed at the beginner/younger crowd. These newer CAD programs have tools that enable even the most innately talentless among us to create with ease.

History of CAD

Let's take a step back and look at what CAD is and how it has developed. CAD used to stand for "computer-aided drafting" as the earliest programs were simply an attempt at helping architects and other engineers with drafting. According to digitalnews.com, Patrick Hanratty invented the first CAD software program in 1957. He worked for GE (General Electric) at the time, and his program was called PRONTO, which stood for Program for Numerical Tooling Operations. As 3D printers would not be developed for another thirty years, his program was used to operate CNC machines.

Recall that CNC stands for "computer numerical control." CNC devices are a type of **CAM** machine. CAM stands for "computer-aided manufacturing" and covers a wide range of machines, including 3D printers, CNC machines, and many others that are controlled by software. You will often hear of CAD/CAM together in the same sentence as you can't really have one without the other. A machine with no file to run it isn't really going to do much, and while it is fun to examine 2D and 3D designs on a computer, you can't really do much with them without a machine to make what is in the files.

Some companies have tried to combine CAD and CAM into one software package. CAD/CAM software allows you to design a program in CAD, and then the design will control the machines that make the part. Mastercam is an example of this. Long a leader in CNC CAM software, it has partnered with Solidworks to create an integrated package that allows you to develop your model and prepare the **toolpaths** for it to be cut out. As of the writing of this book, I am unaware of any software packages that allow you both to create your digital file and slice it for a 3D printer. I am sure they are on their way, but for now the two steps are separate and distinct. This chapter will focus on CAD, while we will discuss slicing software in the next chapter.

Continuing our story of how CAD was developed, it was in the 1970s that CAD programs went from 2D CAD to 3D CAD. Three-dimensional CAD programs are so prevalent today that when someone refers to CAD they are most likely referring to 3D CAD, but that was not always the case. Universities and large corporations usually developed the early CAD programs, and they required large mainframe computers to run on. Thus the price of these programs was out of reach of most users. The main users of CAD software at the time were automotive and aeronautical manufacturers. They could afford the software and associated hardware, and they had a need for sophisticated engineering programs with which to model and test their designs. It wasn't until the PC revolution of the 1980s that CAD programs could be brought to the average consumer.

Windows and early Apple operating systems were not powerful enough to handle the requirements of CAD, so the first CAD software packages were based on the UNIX operating system. It wasn't until 1983 that a company called Autodesk developed AutoCAD for the IBM PC. This event started an avalanche of CAD software programs like Rhinoceros 3D, Solidworks, Inventor (also by Autodesk), and many others.

Finding 3D Files to Print

Before we even begin to discuss using 3D CAD software to create digital files for slicing and printing, there are much easier methods to consider.

The first of these is to look on your 3D printer itself. Either loaded on the firmware or placed on an SD (secure disk) card are usually a bunch of files that the printer can print right away. More often than not, a 3D printer will contain a test print—such as a simple cube—to make sure that the printer is functioning properly. It is always a good practice to start with a simple test print due to the fact that errors can be time consuming and messy.

My Dremel 3D20 Idea Builder comes with the following stock files:

1.   Child's Dice
2.   Rhinoceros Head
3.   School Bus
4.   T-Rex Head

5. Toothpaste Squeezer
6. Reindeer Puppet
7. Polar Bear Puppet
8. Dremel Test Print (a cube with the Dremel logo printed on it)

These are two of the stock prints that come loaded on the Dremel 3D20 SD card: a rhino head and a cube.

That Place Called the Internet

Beyond what is available on the printer itself or an attached SD card or flash drive that comes with the printer, you should look on the manufacturer's website. For example, on the Dremel site there are approximately 240 designs available to download. There is no charge; you just have to be registered on the site. These designs fall into several categories, including education, entertainment, gadgets, home, etc. Among some of the cooler things I've found on its site are a world map, a catapult, chess sets, a twenty-sided die, and a frog pencil topper.

One advantage of downloading files from a 3D printer's site is that the models are optimized to work with that specific printer. All you need to do is load one up in a slicing program and hit print. It should be the right size and have the correct settings all ready to go. But where there are literally tens of thousands of designs waiting and ready for you to download, modify, and print is our wonderful friend the World Wide Web.

The internet is chock full of sites hosting 3D print files for your use. If you were to search for these sites, like anything nowadays you would get a million or more hits, the majority of which would be useless. As you start to search and research, you will soon begin to recognize which sites are good and which are bad. You may find downloads from one site don't work very well or convert to the file type you need, or you may discover that when you print items off of a particular site, they don't work very well or always seem to clog when printing or break after you're done.

The sites you visit will fall into roughly two categories: those that offer a large repository of files for free, and those that have a few free ones along with many you can purchase. While at first I balked at the idea of paying for 3D print files, I noticed that some of the print files for purchase were really outstanding or unique in some way or were just really well done. Here are five sites with a quick description so you can get an idea of what is available.

1. Thingiverse (https://www.thingiverse.com): This site is the absolute biggest repository of free 3D print files out there. The scope and breadth of what it has available is staggering. Originally designed as a companion site for the MakerBot 3D printer, it offers no limitations on who can use it; you don't even have to have an account on the website to download an .stl file (a stereolithography, or **STL**, file generated by CAD software). A quick perusal of the site shows spaceship models, screws, organizers, cookie cutters, and the subject of chapter 5: fidget spinners! There are hundreds and hundreds of fidget spinner designs, and literally thousands of other print files as well. This is the place to start, and you may actually never leave.

2. Pinshape (https://pinshape.com): A mixture of free and for-sale items can be found on this site. While not as populous as Thingiverse, the items it does have seem to be a bit more intricate. There are a lot of characters and creatures, and dragons and Death Stars, as well as cosplay masks and weaponry for the next convention you're going to.

3. Sketchfab (https://sketchfab.com): Strictly speaking, Sketchfab doesn't just offer 3D files to download for printing. It hosts everything

3D, from animations to virtual reality and 3D sketches. The stuff on this site is out of this world and really high quality. It has artists in residence as well as community contributors.

4. MyMiniFactory (https://www.myminifactory. com): This is a curated site, meaning it doesn't host just any file for download. Instead, it chooses which files to host. The downloads, however, are free. Generally you get higher quality items on here, though the quantity is certainly less than a site such as Thingiverse. It does host ads for 3D printers and accessories, which is something I haven't seen on the other sites, but the ads aren't intrusive or overbearing.

5. Yeggi (http://www.yeggi.com): I included this site because it is different from the others. It doesn't host files on its own. Rather, it is a search engine that finds files in whatever category you wish and displays links to the sites where you can find those files.

With computers and modern technology, there is always a new or different way to accomplish a task. The methods above (using preloaded files, using files provided by a printer company on its website, and using a community-created site that hosts files) are the main ways to get STL files for 3D printing. Once you have exhausted those methods, you can't find what you are looking for, or you've just decided it's time to get started creating on your own, then it's time to take a look at creating with 3D CAD.

Parametric and Direct Modeling

All the programs mentioned at the end of the section on the history of CAD (Inventor, Solidworks, etc.) are called **parametric modeling** programs, and this is an important term for us to understand. Parametric modeling refers to the ability to create dimensions and other specific constraints on parts of a model so that by changing one part, you affect the entire model. Parametric modeling usually involves starting from scratch with a sketch or drawing that is then developed into a 3D design through the **extrusion** of shapes into parts, the combination of those parts into new shapes, the addition of constraints to those parts so that they lie in specific configurations in the shape, and the addition of features like chamfers, fillets, holes, and others. Parametric modeling allows for very sophisticated models that have very specific features. If you change the dimension on one specific part, it can change the entire model.

Parametric modeling is very important for engineers and others who need to have specific geometric relationships among all the parts and pieces on their models. It allows for features to be located at exact points, and for the thread size for screws to be the right pitch and have the correct threads per inch. However, programs that use parametric modeling are complex and require a significant amount of learning and practice to become fluid with them. As 3D printing has become more popular and accessible, people have wanted to be able to produce shapes and designs without the need for specific geometric constraints.

Direct modeling has developed to meet this need. I have heard direct modeling referred to as the dumbing down of CAD, and I take exception to that term. Both types have their place and their use, and while parametric is more sophisticated, I think it is misleading to call direct modeling "dumbed down." Direct modeling allows for the connection of premade shapes into an overall model. Shapes are combined, but they usually don't have the same geometric constraints or relationships they do in parametric modeling. In addition, you can usually change the size of an object in direct modeling by grabbing the corners and pulling with your computer mouse. In parametric modeling, you don't have that ability as each part of a whole object has its specific dimensional constraints.

Most programs are a combination of direct and parametric modeling styles, with one or the other dominating depending on the purpose of the program. Because they require less computer processing power, CAD programs (called "apps" these days) using direct modeling have proliferated in recent years. These programs are often free, and many of them are web based.

Some of these newer programs are SketchUp, Autodesk 123D Design, Tinkercad, and Autodesk Fusion 360. Before we go on to take a closer look at these programs, I want to lament the absence of a few. Autodesk had put out an entire suite of programs a few years ago for the iPad. 123D Design was joined by 123D Catch, 123D Sculpt, and 123D Make. Each of these was free and easy to use. While no disrespect is intended for Autodesk, I am really upset that they took these programs away. Sculpt allowed you to create monsters and creatures from forms by pulling and pushing on specific parts, then exporting the file for use with a 3D printer. Catch allowed you to take multiple pictures of an object in a circular pattern, like your friend's head, and then it would render that object into a 3D printable file. These tools were easy to use and fun, and were great to integrate with the 3D printer.

I began using Autodesk Inventor, a parametric modeling program, in 2011, well before I had a 3D printer. At the time, I didn't even have a CNC machine or any other type of CAM apparatus. As a teacher (and not an engineer), I barely scratched the surface of a program like Inventor, but I really liked its ability to create exact dimensions and relationships between parts. Most of my students, though not all, found the program very easy to use for the basics but couldn't handle the more complex aspects of the program. They preferred a program like Tinkercad, which uses more direct modeling methods.

The Puzzle Cube

Let me use my puzzle cube project to help compare and contrast Tinkercad and Inventor. Both of these programs export files in the .stl format. This is the format that is read by slicing programs before they export G-code to a 3D printer, but more on that later. The point is both programs (and most of the other CAD programs listed so far) are able to create files that are useable by a 3D printer.

The puzzle cube project is one that is part of the curriculum provided to me by an organization called Project Lead the Way. In the project, students have to design a puzzle made from twenty-seven 0.75-inch (1.9-centimeter) cubes. Their puzzle must have five parts that fit together in a 2.25 × 2.25 × 2.25 cube. Students

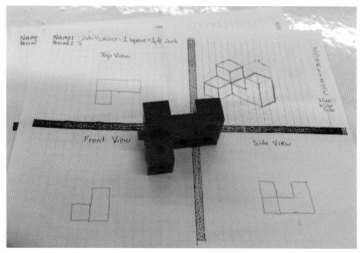

A prototype of a puzzle cube part made of linking cubes. Below that is the isometric (*top right*) sketch along with three sketched orthographic views (top, front, side), which aren't properly lined up.

are supposed to use a direct modeling program like Tinkercad to model their parts, then create different types of sketches (isometric and orthographic) of those parts. When they're done, they can make the parts by gluing wood cubes together or printing out the parts with a 3D printer.

This project leant itself very easily to Inventor. All the cubes were the same size, and they all had flat sides and right angles—lots of right angles. This made them easy to create, line up, and stick together, and made it really easy to change the size. The process was quite simple. Even if you are unfamiliar with Inventor, it shouldn't be too hard to follow the process.

1. Sketch a rectangle and give it a dimension—let's say 1 inch (2.5 cm) by 1 inch.
2. Extrude (pull out) that rectangle 1 inch.
3. You have now created a 1-inch cube.
4. That is considered a part.
5. The next step is to create an assembly.
6. In Inventor, an assembly refers to any item made from two or more parts or other assemblies.
7. Place as many cubes into the assembly as you need to make your first puzzle piece.
8. Stick those together using some commands called "Mate" and "Flush."
9. Mate is a method of sticking two faces together. Flush means to make the edges even, just like in carpentry.

10. Repeat this process four more times for each of the other four puzzle parts, and you're almost done.
11. Create one final assembly wherein you place all five puzzle parts and mate and flush them together.

As in any computer software, it obviously is tougher than it sounds, and there is a learning curve. Regardless, it is pretty easy. I can teach most of my students how to get through this process in a few class periods. However, the project actually calls for the students to use modeling software to prototype their puzzle parts before making them out of wood or 3D printing them. I find that this is too difficult for them to do with Inventor. They can model parts they already have in front of them, but to actually use the software to come up with the parts on their own is very challenging to say the least. That's where a direct modeling program like Tinkercad comes in.

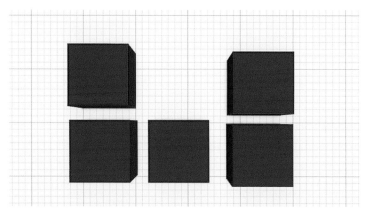

This is a screen shot of five 1-inch by 1-inch cubes placed in Tinkercad.

Tinkercad does not have any of the geometric constraints of a program like Inventor. And you don't have to sketch and extrude shapes. If you want a block, just grab a block. If you want it to be half an inch, just click and make it half an inch. If you want to change that measurement later, it's as simple as clicking on the shape and pulling with the mouse or track pad. And when you want to put the pieces together, there are no tidy constraint tools like the Mate and Flush functions. Instead, you just place the pieces next to each other, visually making sure they line up. Once you have the shapes together the way you want them, you then highlight them and use a "group" tool to make them all one piece.

If you want to compare the process in a step-by-step form with the one in Inventor, it would look like this:

1. Drag a block onto the build plate.
2. Pull the edge of the cube until you make it the desired size.
3. Duplicate the cube until you have correct number.
4. Drag the cubes into the desired positions.
5. Highlight all the cubes and click "Group."
6. Export your model as an .stl file.

My students took to Tinkercad more quickly than I did. I kept trying to do some sort of parametric modeling with the program. I kept fussing over the fact that there was no way to mate the cubes or accurately align them

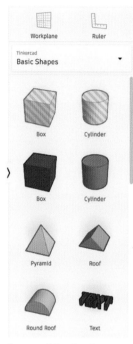

Some of the basic shapes you can start with in Tinkercad

and dimension them properly. Meanwhile, they just dived right in and grabbed a block, dragged it into the build area, sized it, duplicated it so there were five of them, then placed them together. Using the Group function turned all five into one object, and voila! That's all it took, and they did it on an iPad in half the time it would take me on a Windows desktop computer. Also, they did it without the two-week course I took in 3D CAD. Things have changed with the evolution of CAD tools.

Calling Tinkercad a dumbed-down 3D CAD program ignores the fact that it was the right tool for what the students were trying to do. My students were modeling cubes to see if they had the right shapes for their puzzles. To do so, they needed something that was easy to use and quick. Both Tinkercad and Inventor can export .stl files for a 3D printer to use, so the question isn't which is better. The question is which one is more useful? We didn't need the geometric constraints that were provided by a program like Inventor. The cubes stuck together into a shape without them. Instead of a mate or flush to align them and put them together properly, a highlighted blue line would appear on the edges of two cubes when they were in the right place. The process was very simple and very quick.

You can see for yourself in the picture below how the puzzle piece I modeled in Tinkercad came out. You can't really tell what software was used to design it in the first place. A slicing program (in this case Dremel software) was used to convert the exported .stl file into G-code, and I then sent it to my Dremel 3D20 machine.

You couldn't tell which program was used to design this puzzle piece unless you noticed the overlap of parts seen at right.

In the third view of the puzzle cube piece, you can see a small line where the block on top slightly overlapped with the one underneath it. This was because I had not moved it properly and failed to notice that there was no highlighted blue line to show that the blocks were lined up evenly. This was clearly my fault for not checking—as opposed to blaming the software. But in a parametric modeling program like Autodesk Inventor, it would have been very difficult for me to finish the digital model without making sure that all edges were flushed properly. The design of the program just wouldn't allow it.

If you want to make an engine part or a piece with threaded screw holes placed at just the right angle and in just the right place, with just the right width and just the right depth, then there is no doubt about it, a program like Inventor is what you need. But that is not what we needed for this project. In the end, the "better" 3D CAD program is the one that best suits what you are trying to accomplish.

Closer Look at Parametric Modeling

Let's take a closer look at some of the tools that are available to you in a parametric modeling program. First check out the browser history. I recreated the puzzle cube piece I made in Tinkercad using Inventor to show you the complexity of even such a simple design.

I've opened up each part of the browser history for you to see what has gone into this simple model. Each part was made from a sketch and an extrusion, and each of these sketches

A screenshot of the part in Autodesk Inventor shows pieces lining up.

and extrusions had dimensions attached to them. Each part was also mated and flushed with another part in order to create the full puzzle piece. The power of a fully parametric program like Inventor is that I can go back at any time and change a part and the entire assembly would update automatically.

Remember the original project called for 0.75-inch cubes? In the instructions on page 39, I accidentally created a 1-inch cube instead of a 0.75-inch cube like my criteria called for. To fix this, all I would have to do is double-click on the part file titled "Cube" in the browser history, and the full puzzle assembly would gray out while just the cube I chose would be highlighted. I could then adjust the dimensions to my sketch and extrusion to 0.75 inches, and when I was done the screen would go back to the puzzle assembly, only the entire thing would no longer be made out of five 1-inch cubes.

The browser history in most parametric modeling programs is very powerful and extremely important if you need to make changes or discover where you might have made a mistake. Just to make clear the contrast with a direct modeling program, let's take a look at some of the functions that are available in parametric modeling programs.

Let's look at Autodesk Fusion 360 because it is a basic parametric modeling program. "Basic" does not mean that it is simple or easy or limited, it just isn't as fully fledged as a program like Inventor or Solidworks. Still, there is a lot of functionality to contend with.

When you make a model in Fusion, you begin with a sketch. The sketch can be in the form of a line that goes from point A to point B, or a spline or arc, which are types of curved lines. In addition, you can also make closed polygons like a circle or a rectangle. Whatever you sketch, if it is not a closed sketch it will not be able to be modified later on. A polygon and a circle are closed shapes by definition, but lines and arcs and splines must be placed in such a way that they meet and form closed shapes if you are to modify them later on.

One point (no pun intended) I want to make is the inclusion of "point" in the sketch options. I find points very useful when I am designing a 3D model. I use them to help me locate midpoints and other spots on a feature that I may need to use later. You can dimension a point anywhere so you have an exact measurement you can reference later.

Once you have a sketch, you can do a number of different things with it. The simplest is to extrude the figure, which basically means to give it another dimension. For example, a square becomes a cube, and a triangle becomes a triangular prism. You can revolve a shape around an axis; using this method, I take a long, thin rectangle with a right triangle placed on top and revolve around the axis to create a crayon. With the Loft command, you can create a connection between two sketches on different planes. Imagine using Loft to create an ice cream cone shape between a very small circle and a much larger one at a higher plane. You can also add threads to a long rod to create a screw, or you can create a threaded hole to accept screws.

Once you have created a three-dimensional shape, you can further modify it by using the Chamfer or Fillet tools. Fillet is used to curve the ends and edges of shapes. Chamfer is used to cut off corners at uniform angles rather than rounding them. If you've ever picked up a children's toy, you'll notice that there are very few sharp edges. This is obviously to keep kids safe. The edges have been chamfered.

There are a multitude of other tools you can use in a parametric modeling program. I have barely scratched the surface here. One last one that I think we should pay close attention to is the **Shell** tool. If you shell a feature, you basically scoop out all the insides. Basically you go from a solid cube to a hollowed-out box. When you are 3D printing an object, unless you have a need for something to be solid, you may want to consider shelling it. This allows you to use less material, and it will also save you lots of time.

There is no way in one chapter of a book to teach you all there is to know about 3D CAD software. The best way for you to learn is to dive right in and get started. You can begin with a free online program like Tinkercad. It is a direct modeling program that will get you started quickly enough, and it has a multitude of tutorials and training videos you can find on YouTube. If you find that the software is easy to master or not meeting your needs, you can get a thirty-day free trial of Autodesk Fusion 360 or you can try SketchUp or some other parametric modeling program.

In the next chapter, we are going to look at how to take your 3D CAD files and export them into .stl files so they can be used by a slicing program and be prepared for 3D printing.

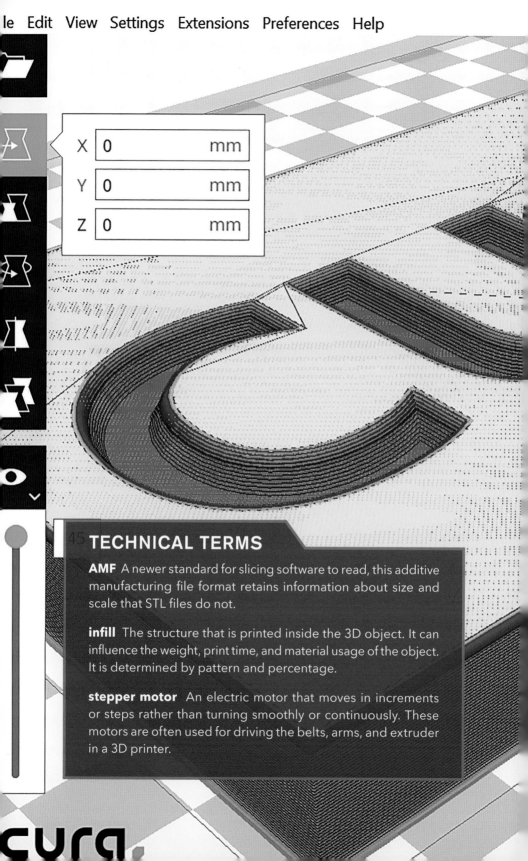

le Edit View Settings Extensions Preferences Help

X | 0 | mm
Y | 0 | mm
Z | 0 | mm

TECHNICAL TERMS

AMF A newer standard for slicing software to read, this additive manufacturing file format retains information about size and scale that STL files do not.

infill The structure that is printed inside the 3D object. It can influence the weight, print time, and material usage of the object. It is determined by pattern and percentage.

stepper motor An electric motor that moves in increments or steps rather than turning smoothly or continuously. These motors are often used for driving the belts, arms, and extruder in a 3D printer.

cura.

CHAPTER THREE

Slicing

THERE ARE NO FANCY ACRONYMS (CAD, CAM, CNC, FFF, etc.) to describe slicing software; the word itself describes what it is and what it does. It slices your digital file into hundreds or thousands of layers and creates a toolpath for your print nozzle to follow. Slicing software is the intermediary between your CAD file and your 3D printer.

We do, however, have an acronym that I have alluded to before but have not explained, STL. In researching this book, STL is said to stand for "standard tessellation language" or in some cases "standard triangle language." However, older sources say that the acronym stands

Opposite: This image of the layer view in a program called Cura shows the layers in which this model will be printed.

for "**st**ereolithography," which both describes the file format and the type of 3D printing process I wrote about in the first chapter's section on the history of 3D printing. These sources refer to the more current meanings as "backronyms," indicating that they derived their names after the fact. Further research bears this out, but you will be hard pressed to find anyone other than an engineer familiar with the history of 3D printing who would be able to tell you that. More important, in common usage, STL is understood to refer to "standard triangle language." This is probably a better descriptor of what it does.

When you create your STL file from a 3D CAD file, the program you are using will read the surface of your file and recreate it in triangles. That may sound strange to you or me, but triangles represent a geometric language that is easy to understand, interpret, and follow for computers and for a computer-aided manufacturing apparatus.

A simple shape like a cube can have each face described by two triangles, but a complex shape like the rhinoceros head I printed out and showed you in chapter 2 can require thousands of triangles to describe the curvature and differing angles and points. Thus, the more complex a design is, the larger the STL file will be.

STL files contain no color or density or similar information. They really only describe the faces of the shape using the x, y, z coordinate system and the previously discussed triangles. Every face that lies at a distinct angle has to be described by two triangles; this makes it very easy for machines to read and then build. Indeed, STL has become the standard file format for most rapid prototyping machines and CNC mills, as well as 3D printers. Since the company 3D Systems invented it in 1987, it has remained relatively the same, undergoing only one major update in 2009 to STL 2.0. It is not coincidental that the development of STL coincided with the development of the first commercial printers for use outside of industry.

There is one alternative to STL that has been gaining some traction in recent years: additive manufacturing file format, or .amf. Commonly referred to as AMF, this standard was developed by the American Society for Testing and Materials, the same organization that created the categories of additive manufacturing machines listed in chapter 1. This file format differs from STL files in three significant ways. It is open source, it uses a different methodology for describing shapes and volumes, and it allows for more information to be output from CAD software than just the shape of the object.

It is probably safe to say that 3D printers and the 3D printing community would not exist—at least in the way they are today—without the open-source community. "Open source" simply means what it says, to openly share the source of all files, documentation, code, etc. The open-source community believes strongly that we are better off when this sort of information is shared. Open source is why I am able to choose from among thousands of different files hosted on Thingiverse. Open source was also the foundation the RepRap community was built upon. My original 3D printer, the RapMan, was developed based on the open-source files shared by RepRap. AMF is open source and will probably benefit from and be a benefit to the open-source community in the future.

AMF also differs from STL in that it does not describe individual faces through the use of triangles. Instead, it uses a more complex geometric calculation to describe the object. The technical specifications are beyond the scope of an introductory book, but the main point to take away is that this new method retains more information than just the shape of the surface, as STL does.

Finally, AMF attempts to tackle some of the future needs that are foreseen with advances in 3D printing. To quote from the standards page released by the ASTM:

> This specification describes a framework
> for an interchange format to address
> the current and future needs of additive
> manufacturing technology. For the last
> three decades, the STL file format has been
> the industry standard for transferring
> information between design programs and
> additive manufacturing equipment. An STL
> file contains information only about a surface
> mesh and has no provisions for representing
> color, texture, material, substructure, and
> other properties of the fabricated target

object. As additive manufacturing technology is quickly evolving from producing primarily single-material, homogenous shapes to producing multimaterial geometries in full color with functionally graded materials and microstructures, there is a growing need for a standard interchange file format that can support these features.

In other words, the world of 3D printing is changing, and the file formats that are being used are no longer supporting the current capabilities of new printers, nor are they enough for the growing needs of the 3D printing community.

While the AMF standard looks promising, I have yet to come across a slicing program that utilizes it, and most files hosted on community sites are still in the STL file format. It will be interesting to see how and if this changes in the near future.

Exporting an STL File

Now that we know what an STL file is, let's look at how to create one. The process is pretty simple and similar across many different platforms. I am only going to cover a few examples, but as with most anything, if you're not sure how to create an STL file with your particular CAD software program, you can always search for the answer in Google.

3D PRINTING A COMPLEMENTARY SKILL

Asking what jobs are available in 3D printing is perhaps the wrong question. A better question would be: What jobs can I no longer do without knowledge of 3D printing? And the answer to that is a great many. An article on Forbes.com analyzed job ads between 2013 and 2014 and found a 103 percent increase in the number of listings requiring 3D printing skills. It found that the jobs requiring 3D printer skills the most were: mechanical engineers, industrial engineers, commercial and industrial designers, and even marketing managers looking to capitalize on the emerging possibilities of 3D printing. The takeaway here is that there are very few jobs that only require 3D printing skills. There are, however, a lot of jobs that require knowledge of 3D printing. And this makes sense. Once you've mastered the basics, there is very little to the actual printing part of 3D printing. You basically set a bunch of parameters and push buttons to make the machine go. It does the rest on its own.

The skills you need to learn to be successful with 3D printing are the CAD skills required to create and design the objects you wish to print out. And these are skills all engineers and designers must become literate with. So rather than say you need to learn 3D printing to get a job, it is more accurate to say that for you to be an engineer or a designer, you need to add 3D printing to your list of skills.

Let's look at two examples to be extra clear on what I mean. I started this book by writing about coral reefs and the desire to print artificial reefs to help replace the dying reefs. While somebody will have to actually operate the machine that prints the artificial reefs, there will also be a need for CAD designers to create the files to print, as well as marine scientists who describe what is needed and make sure that what is designed is helpful and not harmful to the waters in which the reef will be placed. Another area of big promise is that of 3D printing artificial limbs and body parts—in other words, the biomedical field. While printing out parts will be an important function, you will still need the designers and engineers and doctors to make sure that what you are making will fit and function correctly. Again, 3D printing is a very small part of this.

All of this is not to say that 3D printing is not important. It is. It is a highly valuable skill for both home and hobby use and employment. However, you must consider your skills in conjunction with what else you can do and what else you know. In other words, don't just concentrate on 3D printing. Incorporate it into design skills and knowledge in a particular field, and you'll do great.

Tinkercad

There are two ways to create an STL file in Tinkercad. When you are creating a project, you can simply click the Export button and then choose STL as your option. When you log into Tinkercad, you can also go to your saved projects and click "Save for 3D Printing." With either option, you are shown a screen that asks you to choose the file type. Your options are either .stl or .obj, or you can also choose to export in the .svg format, which is a file type for laser cutters and vinyl printers.

Whether you chose either of these options, they will both bring you to the rightmost screen, where you can choose the .stl option.

Fusion 360

While it doesn't specifically state .stl anywhere, this dialog box will save your file as an .stl in Autodesk Fusion 360.

The process is similar in a program like Fusion 360. You just click "File" and "3D Print," and the dialog window at left pops up:

Autodesk Inventor and 123D Design

Autodesk Inventor allows you to choose "Export" from the File menu and then choose a number of options, including .stl. 123D Design is a little different. As it is a cloud-based application, you have to save your file from your iPad to the cloud, then open it on a desktop and download it as an .stl.

There are hundreds of CAD software programs out there, and each one has a similar methodology as to how it exports or saves a file as an .stl. No matter what software package you use, when you export a file as an .stl it will create the triangles mentioned earlier, and the file will look something like the model of Yoda to the left.

If you look closely at this model you can see the triangles created when you export a CAD file as an .stl.

Slicing

There are a lot of slicing programs available, and while some are multiplatform, meaning they can prepare an STL file for more than one printer, the majority of them are printer specific. In the past, I have used a few different ones, and they usually differ in the amount of control they give the individual over settings on the printer and in creation of the build file.

The more familiar you are with 3D printing, the better you will be at fine-tuning the controls on your printer. You can do some of this on your printer, but you can usually control a lot more from your slicing software. From your slicing software you can control the temperature of your printer nozzle for different types of material; heat up your print bed if your printer requires that; control the speed of the printer, the layer height, and the fill percentage; and navigate a whole range of other options like rafts and, most important, supports. We'll look at each of these terms in detail shortly.

3D PRINTING TIP

Slicing software runs the gamut from simple to complex, with the tradeoff being that the more complex the software is, the greater amount of control it gives you but also the more difficult it is to learn. On the other hand, simpler software is easier to use but doesn't give you that much control over your print file.

To learn about slicing software and to see the difference between types of machines, I am going to examine two programs, the Dremel 3D Idea Builder and Autodesk Print Studio. Autodesk Print Studio supports about ten 3D printers, including Dremel's 3D20 and 3D40 models, MakerBot Replicator, Ember (a printer produced by Autodesk), Ultimaker 2, and a few others.

On the other hand, Dremel Idea Builder software only works with Dremel printers. Dremel Idea Builder can be downloaded from the Dremel website with a free account, and Print Studio comes from the Autodesk website, but it is also included for free in the latest version of Autodesk Inventor.

Though I will concentrate on these two, there are many others. For example, Cura software is an open-source free slicing program that is "optimized for Ultimaker printers," which means it works with others but works best with an Ultimaker. Repetier works with any FDM-type (or FFF-type) 3D printer and can support up to sixteen nozzles, which means you can visualize a multicolored object, even if you don't have the printer to print one out yet. Repetier also has the advantage of running off a server, so you can send print jobs via USB, tablet, or smartphone. Skeinforge and MatterControl have been around for a while and are both sophisticated programs with solid reputations. I use MatterControl with my Rostock Max V2 printer and it is an excellent program.

The reason I have stuck with Print Studio and Dremel is because they are both capable of producing good-quality print files, but they also work well with my target audience: eighth graders. This is not meant to imply that eighth-grade students cannot handle sophisticated software; many can. It means that when I am concentrating on a high-quantity workflow but still want individual students to have the experience of slicing the STL files they designed themselves, I have to work with the software that is going to allow them to do that but not take forever so that a class of thirty students can all get to use the printer in a given amount of time.

What Are All Those Options?

When I open my Dremel software and connect my computer to my Dremel printer, I can do almost anything through the software that I can on the interface of the printer itself. I have the options of controlling temperature of the nozzle and of moving the nozzle and print bed back and forth, up and down, along the x, y, and z axes. One important thing that I can do from my Dremel software that I cannot do with Print Studio is update the firmware on the printer.

Updating Firmware

Firmware is an important set of instructions given to a machine to tell it how to run. Robots need firmware, video game consoles need firmware, 3D printers need firmware. As code gets changed or rewritten and as improvements are made, it is possible for your machines to run better, but only if they have updated firmware. The way I update my robots is through the programming software, and so it is with the 3D printer, too. To update the Dremel, I have to open the Dremel software.

Recently I had a clog in the extruder of my printer and couldn't get it unclogged on my own. When I called the help desk I was asked what firmware version I was running (you can read this on the printer's screen), and I swear the customer service representative was trying not to laugh at me. Apparently I had missed a few updates.

When I ran the firmware update, I noticed a few things right away. First, my machine made nice noises. I know this sound silly, but printers can be noisy. A few mechanical beeps and whistles cover up the noise of the motors moving back and forth, and the firmware update improved those sounds so they are a bit more melodic. Silly? Maybe, but in my class the printer is 20 feet (6 meters) from my desk. While writing this book, I sat in front of it while it was printing constantly.

More important, and the gentleman in customer service told me this would be the case, the **stepper motors** that move the print nozzle back and forth move more smoothly and also faster. The updated firmware had sent a different algorithm (set of instructions) for the motor control, and this really improved things. Just watching the printer, I can tell there is a big difference in how the motors move. Especially when printing around a curve, the motors have to move alternating between the x and y axes. They now do this rather quickly, but still without feeling like the sudden stopping and starting of the motors in one direction and then the other was going to shake the machine apart.

Get Your File

When using slicing software, you need to obtain an STL file for it to use. Most likely you have saved a file you designed in CAD and can locate it on your desktop. The Dremel software also has a 3D Online button that you can click to take you directly to the Dremel website, where you can download any of their hosted files. While my printer is currently printing out a large Yoda bust using Print Studio, I have downloaded an airplane to Dremel Idea Builder so we can look at more of the features.

Arrange Your File

You may recall that STL files don't retain meaningful information on color, size, etc. So when you import an STL file into a slicing program you are most likely going to have to scale it. Knowing the dimensions of one part of your file, you can pretty easily adjust the scale so that it fits. One of the nice things about modern slicing software is it will usually put an image of your object within the printer you are connected to or that you have told it you are planning on using. See the two pictures below:

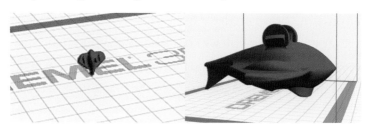

The image on the left shows the plane as the STL file was originally imported. The image on the right shows the same file as I manipulated its size and orientation.

Scale

The first thing I did with the file when I imported it was to scale it. You can usually scale in one of two ways with most slicing software. You can either choose the Scale feature and then grab a handle and drag the object until it looks the right size, or you can type numbers into a box. The default setting for most programs is to keep all the proper proportions, meaning that if you increase the size on the z axis by 10 percent by dragging upward, then the software will increase the size along the x axis by 10 percent and along the y axis by 10 percent.

Move

The Move command allows me to do a few different things with the STL file. First, I can move the image about from left to right, forward and backward, and even up and down. You can theoretically print an object that is hanging in midair. You will just need a lot of supports, but more on those later. I didn't actually want to leave the plane in midair, so I dragged it down toward the build platform. I could also have done this by clicking up and down arrows in a dialog box representing the three axes of direction, x, y, and z.

Your goal when placing an image from an STL file into a slicing program should be to make the object the correct size and to place it in the orientation that will result in the best print, with minimizing use of material being a tertiary concern. So even though I had scaled and moved my plane, I still wanted to do more to optimize it for printing.

Toward this end, there is a Center command within the Move options, and I chose this to center the plane. Next, there was also the option to move it to the platform. As I said before, you don't really want to leave your object hanging in midair. So I chose this option, but it only allowed the fin in the back to touch. This is not ideal because it leaves the rest of the plane hanging in midair. The next option I had was Move Surface to Platform. By choosing this, I was able to double-click on the cockpit of the plane and connect that to the platform. This rotated the plane forward so that the tail fin was again in the air. (Did I mention that the entire plane was upside down?) So I went to the next tool, which was Rotate.

Rotate

With the Rotate tool, I was able to spin the plane in three directions. After a while, I got it to the position you see in the second picture on page 62, with about as much material as possible touching the build platform. This reduces the number of required supports.

Supports

Let's take a look at why Scale, Rotate, and Move are so important. If I was to leave the plane in the air, with only the tail fin touching the platform, it would be awfully difficult to build. That's because the print nozzle on a printer can't print in midair. If it was to extrude filament into midair, that filament would just drop down to the build platform. So you basically have one of three options. You can:

1. Design an object that only has gentle overhangs or even no overhanging parts. If your printer starts in the center and builds outward, only moving upward 0.2 millimeters (0.008 inches) at a time and over even a smaller amount, you can print on an angle because each successive layer will cool and bind to the previous one. If you have too radical of an overhang, or objects that just stick straight out like wings on a plane, this is not an option.

2. You can add supports to your CAD design. In your CAD file you can create supports that rise up from the floor and support parts of the object that are in midair. The amount and placement of these supports is something you will have to work on over time and may take a lot of trial and error.

3. You can use a program that automatically calculates and adds support to your object.

I like option number three the best. The first option is too limiting in that you can basically only design objects in which all parts touch the ground. That isn't really practical. Option number two can work quite well, but you have to know when and where to place your supports and how to build them properly. For an experienced CAD designer, this probably gets easier with time and practice, but for a hobbyist like me it's not practical to use the trial and error method. Therefore I like the third option, which is using software that does it automatically. And this is where I prefer Print Studio to Dremel Idea Builder.

A smaller Yoda (*right*) printed without supports, and that same file (*left*) scaled larger and printed with supports

Keep in mind that I am not here to do a comprehensive comparison of printers or printer software. But as it relates specifically to the adding of supports, I prefer a program that does it for me. Let me show you an example of what I'm talking about.

I don't know for sure how large I could go before I would print an object that would fall over, and I don't want to find out. Print Studio has a great feature that analyzes your model and then asks you if you want to add supports. The answer to this question is always yes.

Print Studio approaches Move, Rotate, and Scale in a similar fashion to the Dremel software, with two major differences. First, Print Studio has a Lay Flat option, which will lay an object flat to the platform. This is a little more robust way of approaching the challenge than trying to rotate and move the object on my own. Print Studio also has an Optimize Rotation option that will spin the object so it is in the best orientation for printing.

Rafts and Skirts

Rafts and **skirts** are two common features of 3D printing. A raft is a layer of filament placed in a rectangular pattern below the printing of the object. The raft layers are usually thinner than the layers of the object. The purpose of the raft is to give the object something to adhere to. Melted plastic filament does a great job of sticking to hardened plastic filament. On the other hand, filament does not always stick to the platform in your printer. I can personally attest to the frustration of watching your print lift itself off of the platform and move when it gets caught on the extruder and has not adhered to the platform. I do have a great work-around for this that I will present to you in chapter 4. I rarely print rafts anymore, but I did print them often when I started.

A skirt is a thin layer of material printed around the object. Usually it is only one layer, and it will encircle your object only once or twice. The skirt serves two purposes. First, it wipes the nozzle clean of any old filament that may have gotten stuck on the nozzle, allowing the filament to flow freely and properly. Second, if you build a tight skirt around the lower layers of your build, it can block the air movement and stop the print from cooling and hardening too quickly.

All Print Options

The screenshot on the next page shows you all the options that you can get from most slicing programs. I will explain what each one is.

"Material" refers to what type of material you are using to build your object. The two most common types in material extrusion machines are **PLA** and **ABS** plastics. Each type has different properties in terms of how hard they are when they cool and what temperature they need to be heated to in order to melt. By setting the type of material, a bunch of other options like extruder temperature are set automatically.

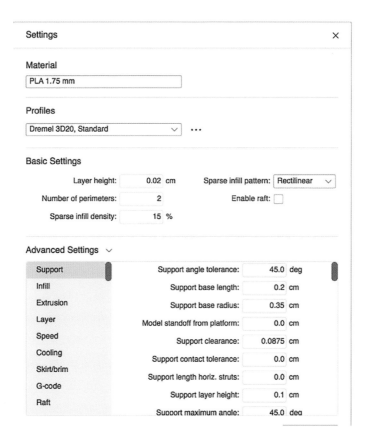

Settings   ✕

Material

PLA 1.75 mm

Profiles

Dremel 3D20, Standard ∨ ···

Basic Settings

Layer height:	0.02 cm	Sparse infill pattern:	Rectilinear ∨
Number of perimeters:	2	Enable raft: ☐	
Sparse infill density:	15 %		

Advanced Settings ∨

Support	Support angle tolerance:	45.0 deg
Infill	Support base length:	0.2 cm
Extrusion	Support base radius:	0.35 cm
Layer	Model standoff from platform:	0.0 cm
Speed	Support clearance:	0.0875 cm
Cooling	Support contact tolerance:	0.0 cm
Skirt/brim	Support length horiz. struts:	0.0 cm
G-code	Support layer height:	0.1 cm
Raft	Support maximum angle:	45.0 deg

Profiles are built for individual printers. Most printers are "plug and play" these days, which means that your software will automatically recognize your printer when you plug it in. The profile will determine a number of different settings for the print in the same way selecting your material did.

Layer Height determines how thick each layer is. The most common layer height is 0.2 millimeters (0.008 inches). A smaller layer height may give you a higher resolution and better-looking builds but will also take longer. Keep in mind that the width of the opening of your print nozzle may limit how small a layer height you can print.

Infill is a very important feature as it can help determine the weight and strength of your build as well as the time it takes to print. The percentage is the overall amount of the inside that is filled, while the pattern refers to the way it looks. There are many patterns available depending on the program. Two more common ones are concentric circles and honeycomb. If you are printing out an item that is purely decorative, then you need a low-percentage infill, but if you want something heavy or strong, then you want a higher percentage. Rectilinear uses straight lines and is easy for a printer to print, but honeycomb is stronger. Concentric circles are good if you are trying to print something that does not have a lot of straight edges.

Perimeters are the same thing as skirt, and I've already covered raft.

Under Advanced are all the things I would leave alone until/unless you become an expert and really know what you are doing. The first of the advanced options is Supports, which we have already discussed. Instead of letting Print Studio add the supports for you, you can adjust the settings for supports. You can choose the length, diameter, base, radius, and many more settings. You can also specify at what angle you want to add supports.

The Infill option under advanced lets you alter the type and amount of infill in different parts of your model rather than just using a uniform amount throughout the entire thing.

The rest of the options let you control how fast your print head moves, how thick different layers are, how much filament is extruded, when and how often the fans come on, and a whole bunch more. Like I said, these advanced options are ones that I wouldn't change unless I had a really good reason to. Their default settings are default for a reason.

Summary

Slicing software has made it easier to operate 3D printers. Before slicing software, you had to convert your CAD file into G-code on your own and then feed it into the printer. That was time consuming and required a great deal of knowledge, far more than the layperson was able to accumulate. Now anyone can create and prepare a file for 3D printing. CAD and slicing programs are freely available and easy to learn and use. And 3D printers are just as easy to use. We'll take a look at how they work and how to work them in the next chapter.

TECHNICAL TERMS

Cartesian printer A 3D printer that moves separately along the *x*, *y*, and *z* axes.

leveling The process by which one ensures the print bed is level, a necessity for creating 3D prints. The process determines that the nozzle is the same distance from the print bed at all points.

thermoplastic Any type of plastic that can be melted at a certain temperature and then regain its original properties quickly after cooling. Thermoplastic makes the ideal material for 3D printer filament.

CHAPTER FOUR

The Printer

I MAY SEEM ODD THAT IT HAS TAKEN ME FOUR CHAPTERS TO get to the point where I am actually talking about the printer itself, but as cool as 3D printers are (and they *are* really cool), they can't do much on their own. You have to have knowledge of CAD and slicing software to get the most out of your 3D printer. Technically you could get away without understanding CAD and just grab a file from Thingiverse, download it, and open it up in slicing software. And even if you don't know much about slicing software, you could keep the default settings, send it off to your printer, and hope for the best. But then again, you might end up with something like the image on page 74.

Opposite: 3D printers can make many cool objects but they can't do much of anything without design and slicing software.

A Boba Fett fidget spinner with flimsy antennae

When I saw this file, I thought to myself, "Oh, what a cool thing to print for my boys, and I can probably use it with the book I'm writing." Well, I'm not giving it to my boys, but I am using it for this book, just not in the way I intended. As soon as I scraped the spinner off of the print platform, I broke one of the antennae. You can see it detached in the picture above. I was able to stop myself and slow down so I didn't wreck the other two, but they are super flimsy and are clearly going to come off on their own after a few spins or just after being stuffed in somebody's pocket.

If I had looked at the CAD file for this, I would have right away recognized that the connection between the helmet and the antenna was way too thin. Even if I didn't have access to the CAD file, the STL file would show me the same problem. I would have adjusted my slicing program to print ABS plastic instead of PLA. ABS melts at a higher temperature but is also much harder when it cools. And while switching the filament on the printer is relatively easy, you have to know how to make adjustments in the slicing software so you are using the right material and heating your extruder to the right temperature.

This chapter will take a really close look at 3D printers. I will cover the names of parts, how they work, how to maintain them, how to fix and troubleshoot them, and how to load and unload filament, and I will introduce you to my secret weapon when it comes to getting the most out of your 3D printer. But please keep in mind that without the background knowledge of CAD and slicing software, you're really limiting your ability to create and shape the world around you.

Filaments: The Big Two

Filament is the material that you are actually using to print your object with. The vast majority of material extrusion printers will use some type of plastic material, most likely **acrylonitrile butadiene styrene** or **polyactid acid** (also called polylactide). I'll refer to them by their common abbreviations, ABS and PLA, and never make you say those names again.

Both PLA and ABS share one important feature in that they are both **thermoplastics**. "Thermoplastic"

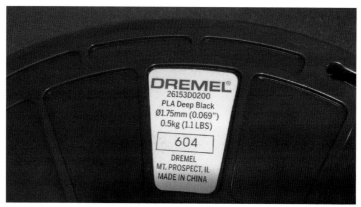

The legend on this filament tells you all you need to know. It was made by Dremel, it is PLA material, the color is black, and it is 1.75 millimeters in diameter.

refers to a material that will become pliable when heated above a certain temperature but will harden when it cools. This is super important because it doesn't melt into a pile of mush, it becomes *pliable*. This means it can be squeezed through the nozzle of the printer without becoming a liquid mess. It will still retain its shape and will harden very quickly after it cools a bit, making the desired solid shape.

PLA and ABS differ in a number of significant ways. PLA is made from corn starch and other plant parts, so it is biodegradable. ABS is derived from oils, and as such it is not biodegradable. Both materials, however, are recyclable.

ABS melts at a higher temperature than PLA. That is true, but do not confuse melting temperature with printing temperature. Melting temperature is the temperature at which a solid will start to deform.

PLA has a melting temperature of 160 degrees Celsius (320 degrees Fahrenheit), while ABS has a melting temperature of 210°C (410°F). The number varies based on the actual composition of the materials; additives like colorants can change the melting temperature, for example. For this reason, some objects printed out of PLA could begin to melt in a locked car on a hot summer day. Printing temperature is what we are more interested in, and that is the temperature at which the material has become molten enough to be extruded through the nozzle and printed with. For PLA that temperature is about 220°C (428°F), and for ABS it is approximately 250°C (482°F). Always check with the manufacturer for their recommended print temperatures.

There are some disadvantages to the higher printing temperature of ABS, but these are offset by the advantages of using it. ABS requires a hotter temperature to print, but that hotter temperature also means less clogging of the nozzle. As I write this, I just had to clean yet another jammed nozzle on my printer. This happens from time to time with PLA. When ABS is extruded onto the build plate, it has a tendency to shrink when it cools, especially if it cools too fast. This causes the edges to curl up sometimes, especially if you don't have good adherence to the print bed.

Due to this, it is not recommended that you use ABS without a heated print bed. Not all printers have print beds that can be heated. And while it is not required, without a heated print bed you will have quick cooling

PLA is prone to clogging as it goes through an extruder due to its lower print temperature.

of your print and a greater chance of shrinking/curling with ABS.

In terms of print quality, items made out of PLA will tend to break a little easier. They also look a little rougher. ABS prints tend to have a little flex to them and are generally stronger than items made with PLA. LEGO pieces are made out of ABS, for example. ABS prints also tend to look a little glossier than PLA prints do.

Other Filament Types

There are numerous other types of materials you can print with. A lot of them are made by adding materials to PLA or ABS, and a lot of them are stand-alone materials. Each of these "specialty" filaments is used for a specific reason, and just like PLA and ABS, each has advantages and disadvantages. While it is difficult to get an accurate count of all the different filament types because there are new ones being developed all the time and because some are just small variations on others, it is safe to say there are more than fifty types of filaments out there. I will briefly examine five of them just to give you some idea.

1. Wood. Yes, really, wood. You're not stuffing a tree into your printer nozzle and hoping it comes out the other end in thin lines, but with the addition of wood fibers to PLA, you can print objects that look remarkably, well, wooden. Wood filament requires no heating bed, but it is not the strongest of materials and does not flex very well. It does, however, look really cool as you can find all types, including cherry, birch, and cedar.

2. Polyvinyl alcohol (PVA) is a substance that is usually printed in conjunction with another material in a dual-extruder machine. PVA is soluble in water and so is often printed as support material to help shape and hold up the actual object. When you are done printing, you can immerse your object in water and the PVA will dissolve away, leaving just the ABS/PLA or other material.

3. As a bicycle enthusiast, I am super excited about this next one because you can print with carbon fiber. Right now all the rage in mountain bikes is the high strength and light weight of carbon fiber parts. You can also get carbon fiber filament

for your printer. It will produce some very rigid, dense, and strong objects. Because carbon fiber is also very abrasive, even as a finely ground powder it can still wreak havoc with your extruder nozzle. You will most likely have to upgrade or replace your nozzle if you're using carbon fiber.

4. A company called NinjaTek (https://ninjatek.com) creates a flexible filament called–what else would you call it?–NinjaFlex. This is a polyurethane material that has quite amazing flexibility and squishiness after it is printed. Imagine being able to print a LEGO connector that you can bend any direction you want.

5. A newer type of filament called nGen is supposed to combine the best of both PLA and ABS. It will print at a wide range of temperatures and is supposed to be successful without refining your print settings. It has a smoother finish to it than ABS or PLA, but it is brittle.

Those are just five of the fifty or more filaments out there. If you are just starting 3D printing, I would suggest PLA because it doesn't require a heated bed and is easy to use. You may also want to look into nGen, but as it is newer, I don't have much familiarity with it. Once you've mastered PLA, try ABS if you can heat your print bed. Compare two of the same prints and notice the differences. Then look at all the other available filaments and choose the one that will do the job you want it to.

3D PRINTING TIP

After opening filament, cut off the first foot of material. This is due to the material being kinked. In order to keep the spool from unspooling, manufacturers will thread a piece of filament through a hole in the spool. This can cause it to kink and not feed smoothly through your extruder.

PLA and ABS are inexpensive, but buying a name brand from the manufacturer can be more expensive. However, you can also get cheaper products if you go cheap. My suggestion would be to do research on the internet. You will soon learn which brands are worth it and which aren't.

One final comment on filaments. A lot of them can absorb moisture. If filament is left out and exposed for too long, you may notice bubbling with your prints. This is due to moisture escaping when you heat the filament. Be safe and keep your unused filament sealed in a ziplock bag.

Path of the Filament

Filament comes on spools so as to make it easy to unwind and feed into the extruder. Usually the spool is mounted on some sort of apparatus that allows it to spin freely and without entanglement or other encumbrance.

Filament is usually guided from the spool through some sort of tubing that is sometimes held in place by a clip or zip tie. The main idea is to have the filament

White ABS filament ready to be fed into the extruder on a Rostock Max V2

feed smoothly the entire way without any resistance. Therefore there should be no sharp bends in the path of the filament.

The filament is guided toward and enters the extruder, where it is pulled down into the heating element and eventually toward the nozzle, where it comes out in very thin strips to build your object. All of these parts—extruder, heating element, nozzle, and others like a fan and heat dissipation fins—together are known as the print head.

An extruder is the part of the printer that actually pulls the filament down toward the nozzle. It accomplishes this by turning a gear with a motor. The teeth of the gear will grip the filament and guide it downward. On the other side of the gear will be either a smooth surface or a roller to help guide the filament.

Extruder and Filament Size

Though all extruders are different, they usually have a spring tension level that, when pushed down, allows you to manually feed filament through the extruder and into the heating element, where it will eventually be pushed out through the nozzle. It's important to understand that the heating element and the nozzle don't pull any filament. Rather, the filament is pulled from the spool by the extruder, and when it passes the gear in the extruder, it is then pushed down. The heating element will warm it to its printing temperature, but its passage out of the nozzle is due to the pressure of the fresh, hard filament

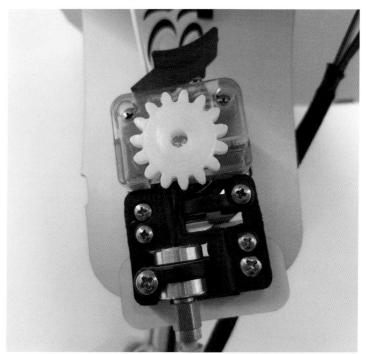

The extruder from a Rostock Max V2.

from above. The nozzle itself is passive; its only mission is to provide a narrow passageway so as to make your printed objects out of lines so fine they bind together and become structurally sound.

The standard nozzle size is 0.4 millimeters (0.015 inches) in diameter. You will find this on most modern 3D printers, though there are exceptions. The other options go down to as small as 0.2 millimeters (0.008 inches), with everything in between. A nozzle of 0.4 millimeters is able to handle most prints in a relatively quick manner. It can print as small as 0.1 millimeters (0.004 inches) in layer height and is relatively clog free. When you use smaller diameter nozzles, they are more prone to clogging unless you use the highest quality ABS or similar filament. On the other hand, a small-diameter nozzle can handle really tiny prints with high resolution, and it can go around corners and tight curves better than a larger-diameter nozzle.

You also have a choice when it comes to filament size. Filament originally came in 3-millimeter (0.12-inch) diameter, but in recent years it has given way to the more popular 1.75-millimeter (0.07-inch) diameter. There is not much difference between the two—they both get the job done—but the move to the smaller diameter occurred because it took less torque for the extruder motor to pull through filament that was almost half the size and half the weight. While I say there is not much difference, you can search the internet yourself and find many impassioned arguments in favor of one type or another.

Print Bed

The surface on which the filament is extruded is called alternately the print bed or the platform. To be clear, a surface that lowers and raises along the z axis I refer to as a platform, and one that stays still I call a print bed. In more sophisticated printers—those that are designed to print different filaments—the print bed can be heated. The Rostock Max V2 is an example of a 3D printer with a heated print bed.

Cartesian and Delta Printers

For the print head to extrude the spooled filament, heat it, and print it in a shape that has three dimensions, something has to move. There are two basic ways that printers accomplish this. Delta printers have three or more arms arranged equidistantly from each other and from a center point in the circle they describe; attached to the end of these arms is the print head. The arms move up and down simultaneously, thus making movements along the x, y, and z axes all at the same time. Delta printers are relatively fast because the arms can all move at the same time. Because of their profile, they can often print taller objects than most **Cartesian printers**.

Cartesian printers move the print head along each axis separately. There are different combinations to cause this movement. For example, the platform can move up and down while the print head travels along the

CLEARING CLOGS AND CLEANING THE EXTRUDER

One of the more frustrating things about 3D printers is when the nozzle gets clogged. When you get a clog, follow precisely the manufacturer's instructions on how to unclog the machine. Most companies usually have PDF files that explain in detail how to clear the clog, as well as YouTube-style videos that show you what to do. If you still have stuck filament or a clog, search for videos from the 3D printing community that show you how to go further than the manufacturer does. Caution: if you take your machine apart beyond the manufacturer's instructions, you may violate the warranty.

I had a clog that I could not get out even after following the manufacturer's instructions. The apparent cause of the clog was filament that did not adhere to the build surface getting stuck underneath the nozzle. This caused it to get backed up and stop flowing. Once things cooled, there was filament stuck in the nozzle. I tried heating the nozzle and pushing the filament through, but that did not work.

Dremel suggested that I heat the nozzle, remove what filament I could from the extruder, and push any remaining filament down out of the nozzle with an unclogging tool. When this failed, I searched YouTube and found a user named RedHair Tech.

He had videos that demonstrated how to take apart the print head so you could remove the extruder and clean/unclog it. The first step was to remove two hex-head bolts to get the fan off. Removing the fan exposed the heat dissipation element, which could then be removed. This exposed the extruder. By removing some tiny Phillips screws, I could take it apart. When I looked at the extruder, I noticed that there were several colors of plastic bits on the gear that is supposed to pull down the filament. So I used a wire brush to clean gunk out of this gear, heated the heating element to 220°C (printing temperature), and stuck the tool down the hole to the nozzle again. This time, because I didn't have to go through the gunked-up extruder, I was able to push out whatever remaining filament was clogged in there.

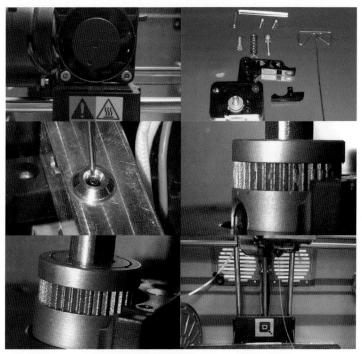

From left to right by row: fan in front of extruder; disassembled parts; poking the cleaning tool through the heating element; the gunked-up gear; the clean gear; free-flowing filament.

x and *y* axes. Or the print head can move up and down along the *z* and also along the *y* or *x*, with the platform moving along whichever axis is left.

Regardless of which type of printer you have, Cartesian or delta, they have some things in common. Both will use stepper motors–to move the arms on a delta printer or to move the print head along what's called the gantry in a Cartesian printer. Stepper motors are a type of DC motor that can move in very discrete increments. When controlled by a computer, they can be precise to a tenth of a millimeter. This is what you need in a 3D printer. In a delta-style printer, you will find the arms are raised and lowered by belts that are moved by stepper motors. In a Cartesian printer, the movement along the *x* and the *y* axes is accomplished in a similar fashion, but the raising and lowering of the print head or platform is usually accomplished by one or more large lead screws. A lead screw turns circular movement into linear movement and is not prone to slippage. This

This limit switch was placed to stop the movement of the print head along the *x* axis.

makes them ideal for raising and lowering a platform in a printer.

When the print head or the arms on a delta printer move, they are stopped from going too far by a limit switch. These little switches are easily activated with a slight push. They are also used to help bring the print head to a home position, from which it starts for every build.

Leveling the Platform/Print Bed

A lot of great care has gone into the design of a 3D printer. Filament is extruded and pushed out a hot nozzle in an almost liquid form, but it cools and hardens in mere seconds. A shape is traced as stepper motors move the print head about and layers are added a fraction of a millimeter at a time until the object is complete. This entire process will not work correctly if your print bed is not level. The print bed must be absolutely flat so that the print will come out right. The stepper motors have a home position they always send the print head to. From this position, the printer knows exactly how far it is to the print bed. That is, unless the print bed is not where it is supposed to be—if it's not level.

By level, I don't mean if it looks flat to the naked eye. Level means it is not even a fraction of a millimeter off. Recall that the average layer height in a print is 0.2 millimeters (0.008 inches), so if you are not level by anything more than that, then you are running a chance of having a bad print. Luckily there is an easy way to level most printers.

You can operate the **leveling** function either through slicing software or through accessing the control panel on the printer itself. Whichever method you choose, you can easily level your machine using only a piece of paper. Folded in half and then half again, an average piece of printer paper is about 0.03 millimeters (0.001 inches) thick. Most printers come with a thick piece of paper with the logo of the company printed on it that you can use for leveling. I always lose mine, but there's always a piece of paper available.

When you run the level function, your printer will send the nozzle to three or four different places on the printer, usually the corners and the center. Each time it will move toward the print bed, and this is where you place the paper, between the print bed and the nozzle. Once the nozzle has stopped moving, try to pull the paper out. It should not move easily, but it should not be so tight as to rip—there should just be a little bit of resistance. There are adjustment screws at each corner of the print bed. Raise or lower the bed using the screw in the corner you are testing until you get the desired

3D PRINTING TIP

Before starting to level your print bed, heat the bed to the printing temperature of the material you are going to use. Heating the bed will cause it to expand. Leveling the bed when it is heated will set your nozzle at the right distance from the bed under printing conditions.

resistance. When you do, push a button and the nozzle moves to the next spot. Repeat this action until you have done all the points on the print bed, making sure that the resistance is the same each time. And now you have leveled your printer. I usually perform this action after every four or five prints, but as you get to know your printer you will learn how often you have to level it.

Adhering to the Print Bed

One of the biggest problems encountered with 3D printers is getting the filament to adhere properly to the print bed. A concurrent problem is your print sticking to the print bed too much and not coming off when you are done.

This problem does not occur as often with heated print beds because the material doesn't cool and harden as quickly. However, once it does cool down it can be difficult to take off. The letter-N fidget spinner below shows a project that didn't stick to the print bed.

This N-shaped fidget spinner was printed with PLA. Its defective corner was caused by a failure to stick to the print bed.

Depending on whom you talk to, there are a number of ways to make sure your print sticks to the print bed but comes off easily when you want it to. Some people swear by painters' tape, while others suggest spraying the bed with hair spray before you start. I have my own favorite method that has worked almost flawlessly for me. I use glue.

Specifically, I use Elmer's Disappearing Purple Glue. This magical stuff does a wonderful job of first sticking to the print bed and allowing the print to stick to it. After it's done, the glue dries and "disappears," allowing you to remove the object from the print bed.

Tools Tips

There are a few tools I find indispensable when working with my 3D printer. Some of them came with my printer, and some of them I got myself. The first of these tools is the unclogging tool. The diameter of this tool has to be really small so that it can fit through the extruder hole and push any clogged filament out of the nozzle. For its tiny diameter, it is actually quite stiff, and the little circle at the top helps me to pull stray filament from the end of the nozzle after a print is done. Almost all of the bolts on my Dremel printer are hex bolts, so I keep the appropriately sized hex key around. My Dremel came with a plastic scraper for removing prints from the print bed. I have found that this is inadequate. It bends and flexes when I push it too hard against a stubborn print. My Rostock came with a long metal scraper, and that worked really well. So I looked online and found some similar tools for a really inexpensive price. They were marketed as "3D Printing Accessories," but when my wife (the artist) saw them, she just chuckled and told me they were tools for working with clay. Either way, the shorter metal one is my go-to tool for removing prints from the print bed. Finally, I use a pair of needle-nose pliers to remove filament from the top of the extruder if it's stuck.

In this chapter, I have traced the route of the filament from spool to print bed. We have covered all the major parts of the printer and looked at how they worked together. I have presented you with troubleshooting tips and shown you how to take apart your print head and clean your extruder. And I've described to you the magic of Elmer's Disappearing Purple Glue. In the final chapter, I'm going to show you the process I go through from start to finish to accurately measure, sketch, design, model, slice, and print a fidget spinner.

Tools of the trade: an unclogging tool, a hex key, scrapers, and needle-nose pliers

TECHNICAL TERMS

bearing A machine part in which another part turns or slides.

bevel To create a sloping edge where a straight edge had previously existed.

caliper A precision measuring instrument that is used to measure items down to the thousandth of an inch. A caliper can measure height, width, depth, diameter of the outside of a circle, and the inside diameter of a circle.

CHAPTER FIVE

Let's Print

THE FIRST THING I EVER DESIGNED AND PRINTED WITH A 3D printer was a triangular piece of plastic about 3 inches (7.5 cm) long, 0.5 inches (1.25 cm) wide at one end, and tapering down to about 0.125 inches (0.3 cm) wide at the other end. It was about 0.125 inches high. Doesn't sound like much, but I was really excited.

The reason I printed such an oddly shaped piece of plastic is because I was asked to. The manager of my school's cafeteria came down to my room and asked me for it. She was concerned because one of the food shields—those large pieces of clear plastic that protect food from being attacked by germs from the mouths of

Opposite: Here are several spinners designed by Aaron Maurer and his students.

eight hundred middle school students—had developed a crack in it where it met a supporting piece of metal. These hoods perform an important safety function and are not cheap as they are made out of molded plexiglass.

Instead of purchasing a whole new shield, she was hoping that I could print a piece of replacement plastic for her. So I opened up my CAD software, designed the piece, exported it as an .stl file, sliced it in a slicing program, and printed it out with my Rostock. It was small and not very impressive looking, but it was functional, and I made it. It was a good feeling to find someone who needed help and to provide it to her.

People can get great benefits from 3D printing. You can print a small piece of plastic to fit in a crack on a plexiglass food shield, or you can print a functional limb for someone who lost his or hers. Like the Cyborg Beast we looked at in chapter 1, 3D printing at home can provide an inexpensive alternative to the medical industry. There are hundreds, probably thousands, of useful things you can make with a 3D printer: soap dishes, cable management clips, drink coasters, cell phone cases, doorstops, measuring cups, gears for a robot, the list goes on and on. But sometimes, as the song goes, you "just want to have fun."

If you're a student between first and twelfth grade or a teacher, then you are familiar with fidget spinners. They are those toys that mimic the action of a gyroscope as you spin them faster and faster and pinch the center between your thumb and forefinger. They appeared about

February of 2017, and if I know my fads, nobody will be interested in them by the summer of 2018. But in the meantime, it seemed as if every student of mine had one or wanted one. What I had was a pre-engineering class with an open curriculum and a 3D printer. So I decided it was time to print some fidget spinners.

A great deal of the information in this chapter and my original project came from Aaron Maurer. He runs a website called Coffee for the Brain (http://coffeeforthebrain.com), which covers many education topics and focuses on STEM applications. Recently he posted a tutorial on using Tinkercad to design a fidget spinner for 3D printing. A lot of my initial understanding of this topic started with his website. So if you're ready, follow along, and with the right tools and equipment—and a little bit of practice—you too can make your own fidget spinner.

Usually the first step in designing an item for 3D printing is to sketch the item. However, as fidget spinners are flat and their defining characteristics are holes to accept the **bearings** and weights, I skipped this step and went right to acquiring accurate dimensions. To successfully design a fidget spinner, there are two dimensions you need: the outside diameter of the typical bearings that are used, and the distance between your thumb and forefinger and the webbing of your hand. The diameter of the bearing should be obvious. However, after a few false starts I decided that my students needed to measure their hands. The measurement from the center of the spinner to any outside edge can't be longer than the distance from where they pinch to their webbing, or there won't be room for the spinner to spin. It will keep hitting the webbing. A few of my students didn't take this into account at first and printed spinners that were too large to rotate in their hands (I'm guilty of this as well), so I mandated that they measure this distance first.

Whenever you are measuring something where precision and consistency is important, you should use a set of **calipers**. Calipers are instruments that are designed to measure an item down to the thousandth of an inch. That is extremely tiny, and most of us will never need to measure something that small. The way I explain it to my students is that if you went to an eye surgeon to have laser surgery on your eye, you would want the surgeon to be very exact indeed. I mean spot on or else.

While it is vitally important in certain circumstances, like the one described in the previous paragraph, to be accurate to a thousandth of an inch, in this situation I am going to be satisfied with a hundredth of an inch. The primary reason is that Tinkercad only allows me to design objects to a hundredth of an inch—if you put in a thousandth measurement it will round to the nearest hundredth.

Working with Dial Calipers

Dial calipers are fairly simple to use. They are a bit harder to read. In the picture at the top of page 99, you'll

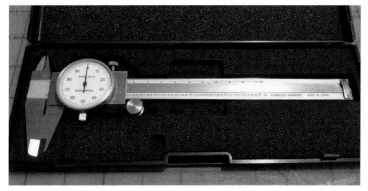

A standard dial caliper with thumbscrews at the top and bottom

notice two thumbscrews and a dial. By gripping the long rectangular bar (called the blade) in your right hand and using your thumb to roll the round piece below the bar (called the fine adjustment roll or clamp screw), you open up the reference faces to the left of the dial, and you can place objects in between them to measure.

In the picture below, the caliper is opened and a bearing is placed between the outside reference faces.

The standard bearing for a fidget spinner is shown between the outside reference faces of a dial caliper.

I have kept the bearing in for illustrative purposes. For actual measurements I would tighten the thumbscrew on top of the dial, and that would hold the reference edges in place. Then you can remove your object and pick up your caliper to read without worrying about it slipping and changing your reading.

To read the caliper, I am going to start with the numbers on the blade to the left of the dial. These are my whole inches and tenths of inches. You can see the zero placed on the blade higher than the other numbers. This is where the whole numbers are placed. In this instance, you can't see any other raised numbers on the blade to the left of the dial, so we can conclude that we have a diameter that is less than one whole inch.

After our whole inches, we can start measuring the tenths of inches. These are also on the blade to the left of the dial, and here is where reading can get a little confusing. It looks like the diameter measurement is nine-tenths, but it is actually eight. You don't count the tenth until you can see the line past the number. It's like when you're learning to read a clock and it's 4:58. A lot of kids will see the small hand really close to the five and say it's five o'clock, when in actuality it's not quite there yet. It's the same with the caliper. It's not quite on the nine, so we don't count it yet.

After reading the tenths of an inch, you look at the dial from which the caliper gets its name. The dial will tell you the hundredths and thousandths of an inch. And you read it just like that. In this case, the dial is right on

68, so our whole reading is 0.868. The diameter of the bearing for our fidget spinner is 0.868 inches (22 mm).

Applying Math

I think I have already made my preference for a program like Autodesk Inventor over Tinkercad clear. There is so much more you can do with fully fledged CAD software over some of the easier-to-use web-based stuff. But let's not forget that it is easier to use for a reason. It has a lower entry point and small learning curve. It also does a lot of dimensioning for you. In the case of our fidget spinner, Tinkercad provides us with some simple mathematical equations to apply in order to start designing.

The diameter of our bearing is 0.868 inches, but in Tinkercad there is no sketch to work with to apply that dimension. Instead, you have to look at what it does offer in the way of the beginner shapes. For the purposes of our spinner, we're going to start with the tubes. The tube is the shape that is most similar to the open holes we want to place our bearing into. The tube offers some different shaping options as well. It allows us to choose how many sides we want for the tube, and how many segments we want to **bevel** and to what extent we want to bevel them.

"Bevel" means to reduce a square edge to a sloping edge. The Bevel Segments option refers to how many separate edges I want on the side of the tube from top to bottom, and the Bevel option lets us decide how much we want to bevel each of those sides. In each of these cases, I've chosen the maximum option (sixty-four sides, a bevel of 0.2 inches, and ten bevel segments). You'll notice that the tube I've created is quite rounded—that's why I chose the maximum option of sixty-four sides—and that's the way I want it. You can experiment with these options yourself to get the look and feel that you want.

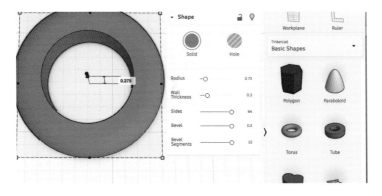

The picture above shows the tube I created using different options in Tinkercad. If you look on the right you can see in the original tube the top is flat and the outsides are straight. Though it is not clear in the model I created on the left, I used the bevel options to slope the top and the bottom to create a more rounded side.

Let's take a look at the other options that pop up when I click on the tube. The top two are Radius and Wall Thickness. Remember our 0.868? This is where that number is going to come in really handy. I want the diameter of my bearing to be the diameter of the inside of the tube so the bearing fits in it. When I first started this process, I used the ruler to measure that distance, but that was never quite exact because it was hard to find two points for the ruler that represented exactly where the diameter was. In my brain, I was still thinking about how I would do this with a parametric modeling program as opposed to a direct modeling program.

Instead of measuring the diameter, I had a lot better luck using the provided options. The wall thickness I put in as 0.3 inches. This was chosen through a little trial and error. I wanted to have walls that were thick enough not to break but that still had a thin profile. So I chose 0.3. If you imagine the diameter of our tube as stretching all the way across the tube, you will pass the wall twice, once on each side. So if we add the two wall thicknesses (0.3 + 0.3 = 0.6) to our bearing diameter (0.868 + 0.6 = 1.468), we have an overall diameter of 1.468. The option Tinkercad gives us is for the radius, which as we know is half the diameter (1.468 / 2 = 0.734). The radius I input is 0.73. Remember, Tinkercad doesn't allow for a thousandth of an inch, and it would be immaterial anyway because the nozzle on my printer isn't narrow enough to print in the thousandth-inch level of detail. I chose 0.73 and not 0.74 because I would prefer my hole to be a little too small rather than a little too big. I can always take material away from a print, but it is much harder to add it after the fact.

The final measurement I made for my spinner is the height. When I used my calipers to measure the height of the bearings, they were 0.275 inches, and so that's what

I made each tube. You can see that in the image on page 102, right on the center of the tube, where I clicked one of the handles to enter the height.

Now that I have my basic structure, I can start to make my spinner. To begin with, I tried the most basic design I could. I duplicated the tube three times for a total of four and arranged them in the classic spinner configuration. When you do this, make sure that you don't overlap the tubes too much, or one will run into the next and you won't have a clear circle for the bearings.

The simple design for a fidget spinner on Tinkercad resulted in a usable model.

From Tinkercad to Final Print

This basic design for a spinner works very well. Without getting too deep into the physics of it, your bearing in the middle that you will use to spin around needs to be the center of mass. By having the three others placed equidistantly around the center one, you are still keeping the center of mass where it needs to be. Thus, any design for a fidget spinner needs to keep the weight distributed equally around the center. This doesn't mean that every print you design will have to be totally symmetrical; the weight will be supplied by the bearings (or coins, or marbles, or whatever you decide to use), not the plastic you print with. You can have a little bit extra plastic on one side or the other and it won't make a lot of difference if your weights are spaced properly.

Using your CAD software, you can take this basic setup and add any details you want to make all sorts of different spinners. Take a look at a few of the designs my students came up with:

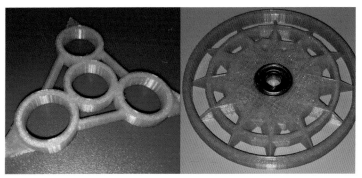

Examples of fidget spinners designed by middle-school students

As we already know, designing an object in CAD is only one part of the entire process. We still have to export an .stl file, slice it, and then send it to our 3D printer. After that, there may still be a few steps to take after printing before we're totally done.

Exporting and Scale

Any software will let you save a file with a file extension that can be read by that software. At least I can't think of any software that lets you save a file that you can't use later; that would make no sense. For example, a design made with Autodesk Inventor will have a file extension of .iam or .ipt, standing for "inventor assembly" and "inventor part" respectively. But slicing software can't read those file extensions or any of the other hundreds that are saved by whatever CAD program you are using. Instead, you need to use the aforementioned .stl file extension. To get this, you have to either export the file or use the option that some programs have called "Save for 3D Printing" or some similar phrase, which in essence means the same as exporting.

Once the file is exported, you can open it in slicing software. Back in chapter 3, when we went over slicing software, I briefly mentioned scaling your design. The example I used in that section was a toy airplane. When I mentioned scaling it, I was just talking about getting the right size visually so that the final print would be generally the size we want. But with something like a fidget spinner, size really does matter.

I mention this because when I import my STL file and open it in Autodesk Print Studio, it is too large to use. It is actually so large it won't even fit on the print bed. When you receive the error message that your file is too large, a pop-up window that asks if you want to scale the image accompanies it. The pop-up window has two options: it allows you to enter a scale factor in terms of percent, or it allows you to choose between inches, centimeters, and millimeters. I designed the file in inches, so naturally I choose that option first, and the size is way off.

I experimented a little bit and chose millimeters instead, and this worked just fine. I was able to use the ruler tool in Print Studio to double-check this method by measuring the inside diameter of each hole, and they all came out to 0.868 inches. In the course of researching and writing this book, I have reinforced things I knew and discovered new information. I don't often come across something I was able to get to work without really knowing how or why I was able to do it. And I don't enjoy not being able to fully explain something to my readers.

Scaling a file that is too big for your printer

If you recall, STL files don't contain dimensions the way a CAD file does, but they do have enough data that you should be able to scale to the appropriate size for your print. I don't know why selecting inches did not work; my best guess is that with some slicing software you need to make sure the units are already set to the same ones you used in your CAD program. Changing the units to match after I

3D PRINTING TIP

Make sure you practice and try out different methods to find what works best for you and your particular CAD and slicing programs and specific 3D printer.

imported the file seems to be where I have had the most trouble with scaling.

Setting the Slicer Preferences

Like almost any software you use, the more you become familiar with it, the more you will be able to tweak it. The same is true for slicing software. Most slicing programs are plug and play and will recognize the printer you are using and create a profile for that printer. For example, when I used MatterControl with my Rostock, it had a stored profile that knew the size of my nozzle, the possible print volume (the maximum height, width, and depth available on the printer), my desired speed, whether I wanted a raft or a skirt, and many other details. Most software will allow you to adjust these, but if you're printing similar items, most likely you will want to use the same settings.

The same is true with the filament you're using. You can set a profile in some software so it knows whether you're using PLA or ABS or something more exotic and what diameter of the material you have, what feed rate it works best at, etc. Again, these are adjustable, so you can change any setting that you desire. However, some slicing software is limited in that it only works with printers that have a nonheated print bed. Print Studio is one such program. It connects to a number of different printers (Ultimaker, Dremel Idea Builder, Printrbot, MakerBot Replicator 2, and some others), all of which have in common a nonheated print bed. A heated print bed, you will recall from chapter 4, is required for printing with ABS and some other filaments. When I use Print Studio and it is connected to my Dremel 3D Idea Builder, I really don't need to change a lot of settings. Once I import my fidget spinner STL, I will go through a bunch of steps that are similar no matter what slicer you are using. I will make sure the scale is correct and the spinner is centered; I will lay it flat if it isn't already and optimize the rotation for the best print. Print Studio has one great feature that makes it my favorite for using with students: it analyzes your file and automatically detects if there are any mistakes that need to be fixed. After inspecting the geometry this way, it can also detect if I need any supports and will automatically add them if I desire. This is nice because students often have trouble designing supports, especially in a direct modeling program.

The triangle spinner with the sharp points shown on page 105 is a good case in point. Those points are a lot thinner than the rest of the spinner; they are not touching the ground (or print bed, if you will) and therefore need support so they don't droop down. Having a slicer that can automatically do this is a real boon.

Final Steps Before Printing

I now have my spinner ready, and there are just a few steps I am going to go through before I print. First, I will check the preview of the file so I can see how it is supposed to print out. Print files will show you a preview of the print, specifically the path the print head will follow. Some of them will even allow you the option of seeing any particular layer of the print (remember there can be hundreds or thousands of layers).

This picture shows the print head's path to make the twenty-ninth layer (out of thirty-four) of the fidget spinner I designed in this chapter.

Once I have prepared my object for printing and have previewed it, I will hold off on printing it until I first check my printer. I want to make sure my printer is on and that the correct type and color of filament is loaded. If it is the first print in a long time, I will level the print bed. I will also scrape off any glue remaining from a previous build and will put down a new layer. If my filament is loaded but I haven't used the printer in a while, I will preheat the extruder before I print. I want to make sure that the filament melts and comes out of the nozzle. You should see a little bit melting out when you preheat. If I haven't used the printer in more than a few weeks, I will even unload and reload the filament.

I do this to make sure I have no clogs. Clogs are more common with PLA than most other filament types because PLA heats at a comparatively low temperature.

G-code

My design is done and my file is sliced. I'm ready to send it to the printer, and in reality that is what I would do. I want first to share with you the G-code from this project. We discussed G-code before, with some examples of what different commands mean, but I thought it might be useful to look at a real G-code file connected to an object you have seen designed, sliced, and printed.

1; generated by Slic3r 1.2.9 on 2017-06-04 at 14:12:11

2; external perimeters extrusion width = 0.40mm

3; perimeters extrusion width = 0.48mm

4; infill extrusion width = 0.48mm

5; solid infill extrusion width = 0.48mm

6; top infill extrusion width = 0.48mm

7 1 M107

8 3 2M104 S225 ; set temperature

9 4 G28 ; home all axes

10 5 G1 Z5 F5000 ; lift nozzle

11 M109 S225 ; wait for temperature to be reached

12 G21 ; set units to millimeters

13 G90 ; use absolute coordinates

14 M82 ; use absolute distances for extrusion

15 G92 E0

```
16 G1 Z0.400 F7800.000
17 G1 E-2.00000 F2400.00000
18 G92 E0
19 G1 X61.553 Y60.432 F7800.000
20 G1 E2.00000 F2400.00000
21 G1 X62.020 Y59.965 E2.07847 F1800.000
22 G1 X63.124 Y58.965 E2.25545
23 G1 X63.632 Y58.547 E2.33354
24 G1 X64.829 Y57.660 E2.51052
25 G1 X65.375 Y57.295 E2.58851
26 G1 X66.654 Y56.528 E2.76557
27 G1 X67.237 Y56.216 E2.84412
28 G1 X68.584 Y55.579 E3.02109
29 G1 X69.192 Y55.327 E3.09925
30 G1 X70.599 Y54.824 E3.27675
```

And that's the first thirty lines of code from a file that is fifty-four thousand lines long. As with most computer code, anything written after a semicolon is a comment and not part of the instructions. You can see in line 9 there is the G28 instruction to home all axes, which I described in chapter 1. Other commands set units to millimeters (G21, line 12) or set the temperature to

3D PRINTING TIP

Not all slicing software exports G-code. Some create their own proprietary file formats that can only be read by specific printers. To generate the G-code above, I used a program called Slic3r. Make sure your slicing software and your printer are compatible.

Celsius (M104, line 8). The vast majority of the commands, however, are move commands. G1 tells the print head to move to a specific coordinate (x, y, and z, though e is used in place of z). You can see the incremental movements for the G1 lines of code are very small, moving less than a millimeter in each direction in each line. The F command seen in some spots defines the extrude rate, which is determined by how fast the gear turns that extrudes the plastic above the hot end.

The reason I present the G-code here goes beyond a curiosity. Slicing software can only do so much, and when it is done it exports G-code to a file to print later or sends it directly to a printer. Once it reaches the printer, you have no control over it. When people get to the point in their 3D printing knowledge/experience where they are not satisfied with the way their prints are coming out, they can start editing the G-code. Editing G-code yourself can help overcome a lot of the limitations of slicing

A student is watching and waiting for a print to be done.

software. Of course, you have to know what you're doing. This is the fine-tuning stage, not coarse adjustments, and it takes a skilled hand to be able to do it right.

Now the work is done, and it's time to print. If your CAD design is solid, you slice the model and get all your settings right, and your printer is ready, the rest is just waiting. And waiting. And waiting. One thing 3D printing is not, is quick. It takes a while.

Postproduction

Once your print is finished, there are a number of final steps to take in order to get your spinner just right. First, you want to make sure your bearings fit. I designed my holes a little too small to err on the side of caution. But if they are too small, they need to be enlarged. There are a number of ways to do this; my preferred method is with a round file. Moving the file in and out and around in a circular motion, you'll start to notice lots of little bits of plastic falling off. Be sure to use a mat or something to catch this as it gets everywhere. Stop and check your sizing often; it is easy to file too much off, and then you're stuck.

Once you've filed all the holes to the right size, you may want to paint your spinner. Often we have a limited choice of color filament available to use, but there is virtually no limitation on paint colors. If you are going to paint, do it before you put the bearings in. Resist the urge to sand rough edges if you use PLA. It tends not to look good or get smoother. Once you've completed your finishing touches, you will want to place your bearings.

A print that did not adhere to the bed (*top*); filing the bearing hole (*middle*); a complete spinner with caps and bearings (*bottom*).

When I ordered my bearings, I purchased two hundred on the internet, and when they arrived, they were the right size but not the right type. I got sealed cartridge bearings, which fit but don't spin super fast and can't be greased because they're sealed. I have since learned from my students that the bearings you want for the middle of the spinner are marketed as skateboard bearings. These have removable seals so you can grease the ball bearings and then cover them again. This is what you see in the bottom photo on page 115.

Once you have designed and printed a basic fidget spinner, there are a variety of next steps you can take. Measuring and printing the caps that go in the middle of some spinners is another level. The caps have to have a specific diameter but also a depth so they don't push against each other. This would require you to use the depth measurement on you calipers, which you do by using the end of the blade and holding the caliper upright. It is difficult printing out items so small and precise, so you will have to have a strong command of your printer settings. Perhaps it's time for a different diameter nozzle or to move from PLA to ABS.

We've come to the end of this book, but not to the end of 3D printing. We've barely scratched the surface. The possibilities with 3D printing are endless. From fixing a cafeteria hood to making a child's toy to printing a replacement body part, there really is nowhere you can't go with 3D printing. Will it change our future for the better? I think it already has.

GLOSSARY

ABS Acrylonitrile butadiene styrene; a type of thermoplastic commonly used in 3D printing.

additive manufacturing Any process in which a machine makes an item by adding material rather than taking it way.

axis (*x, y, z*) Refers to the three basic directions of movement: up and down (*z*), left and right (*x*), forward and backward (*y*).

bearing A machine part in which another part turns or slides.

bevel To create a sloping edge where a straight edge had previously existed.

CAD "Computer-aided design" is software that helps in the drafting and sketching of objects, often in 3D.

caliper A precision measuring instrument that can be accurate to the thousandth of an inch.

CAM "Computer-aided manufacturing" is a process by which a machine controlled by a computer makes something.

Cartesian printer A 3D printer that moves separately along the *x, y,* and *z* axes.

CNC mill A computer numerical control device that uses a drill to cut away material.

delta printer A 3D printer with three or more arms that move simultaneously.

desktop printer This term loosely refers to any printer that is designed for home or middle- and high-school use as opposed to university or large manufacturing business use.

direct modeling A type of CAD software wherein you build shapes from previously existing shapes.

export To create a different file type than the native type.

extruder The part of a 3D printer that pulls the filament down toward the hot end and nozzle.

extrusion A common CAD term that means adding a third dimension to a sketched, closed figure by pulling or pushing it along a third axis.

fidget spinner A toy that uses bearings for weight and to spin very fast, causing a gyroscopic movement.

filament Any of a number of different types of thermoplastic that have been turned into long strings and spooled for use with a 3D printer.

fused deposition modeling (FDM) The patented system for 3D printing by extruding material and printing it layer by layer.

fused filament fabrication (FFF) An unpatented and open-source version of FDM.

G-code "Geometric code" is the standard set of instructions that 3D printers read.

infill The shape and percentage of material that will fill the inside of a 3D-printed object.

leveling The process of making sure the print nozzle is the same height above the print bed at different spots, usually the corners and the center.

material extrusion A type of additive manufacturing where material is deposited in layers after being pushed through a nozzle.

nozzle The last part on a 3D printer that the filament passes through at a high temperature before it is deposited on the print bed or object.

parametric modeling A style of CAD software that allows for designing an object from a sketch and in layers that can be referred back to in a browser history.

PLA Polyactic acid; the most common type of thermoplastic filament for 3D printing as it does not require a heated print bed.

print bed The part of the 3D printer on which the object is built.

raft A thin layer printed underneath the object so as to enable it to be easily lifted from the print bed.

RepRap A community dedicated to keeping 3D printing materials, files, plans, and software open source and available to all at no cost.

scale The process of taking an exported STL file and adjusting its size in the slicing program. STL files do not always retain accurate dimensions; this problem is more common with direct modeling CAD programs.

shell A common CAD term that means to cut out a section inside a digital object.

skirt A few layers that are printed around the base of an object, usually to clear the nozzle.

slicing Cutting up a CAD file into horizontal layers that can be printed.

stepper motor A type of motor that moves in small and very discreet increments; often used for driving the belts, arms, and extruder in a 3D printer.

stereolithography The process of turning a 3D CAD file into a series of connected triangles that can be sliced and exported as G-code.

STL The type of file exported by CAD to be used with slicing software.

subtractive manufacturing A method of making an object by taking away material.

supports Parts that are printed to support overhanging areas in a 3D print. These parts are removed when the print is complete.

thermoplastic A type of plastic that melts when it is heated to a certain temperature but hardens quickly upon cooling.

3D printer A machine that prints objects in three dimensions: height, width, and depth.

3D printing The practice of using a 3D printer to make objects that have three dimensions.

toolpath The path the print nozzle will follow while 3D printing.

FURTHER INFORMATION

CAD

All About 3D Printing

https://all3dp.com/1/best-free-cad-software-2d-3d-cad-programs-design

This site provides a chart comparing, and linking to, twenty-two free-to-download CAD software programs.

Autodesk

https://www.autodesk.com

Autodesk is the maker of Fusion 360, Inventor, and other CAD software.

Tinkercad

https://www.tinkercad.com_

Free, web-based direct modeling CAD software. Tinkercad is easy to use. A (free) account is necessary.

Filament and Other Material

Hatchbox

http://hatchbox3d.com

One of the leaders in printer filament. It has PLA, ABS, and specialty types of filaments in all sorts of colors.

MatterHackers

https://www.matterhackers.com

MatterHackers sells over twenty different types of filament, as well as nozzles, extruders, print beds, and other accessories.

Information and Ideas

All About 3D Printing

https://all3dp.com

A site that is, as it says, all about 3D printing. Contains reviews, how-to articles, and advice.

BAZMARC

http://bazmarc.ca

This is the home page of Marc-André Bazergui, designer of a LEGO 3D printer.

Beyond the Instructions

http://www.beyondtheinstructions.com

Project page for the Seshan brothers.

Coffee For the Brain

http://coffeeforthebrain.com

Aaron Maurer's site, where I got my starter information for 3D printing fidget spinners.

Model Hosting

GrabCAD

https://grabcad.com

GrabCAD specializes in 3D printing items for engineering. A quick look at its site shows files for 3D-printed mountain bike suspensions, different screw sizes, shock absorbers, calipers, robotic hands, etc.

Thingiverse

https://www.thingiverse.com

Thingiverse is the place to be for free models to 3D print. Hundreds of thousands are available, and more are being added all the time.

Printer Manufacturers

Dremel

https://3dprinter.dremel.com

This is the site for the Dremel 3D20 and 3D40 Idea Builder. You can learn about their products and download their software here.

MakerBot

https://www.makerbot.com

Long a leader in the 3D printing business, MakerBot makes desktop as well as large-volume 3D printers.

SeeMeCNC

https://www.seemecnc.com

SeeMeCNC specializes in do-it-yourself printers.

YouTube Channels

RedHair Tech

https://www.youtube.com/channel/
UCr3hYzes4SBXGXZsxcgVXJw

RedHair Tech's tutorials on how to troubleshoot
3D printers were indispensable to me while writing
this book.

Skyler DeVault

https://www.youtube.com/user/nanerpus00000

Skyler DeVault is the recipient of a 3D-printed hand
from the Enabling the Future project.

3D Printing Nerd

https://www.youtube.com/channel/
UC_7aK9PpYTqt08ERh1MewlQ_

Joel Telling's channel has hundreds of videos.

INDEX

Page numbers in **boldface** are illustrations. Entries in **boldface** are glossary terms.

ABOUT THE AUTHOR

Ian Chow-Miller is a New York native who has lived in Tacoma, Washington, for the past ten years. He began his career as a social studies teacher but switched to robotics a decade ago and has added 3D printing to his workload. He has written curriculum for robotics and trained teachers around the country. He is a member of the LEGO Educator's Advisory Panel and is a constant contributor to Tufts University's LEGO Engineering website. Ian has coached FIRST LEGO League consistently since 2004, and when robotics season ends, he starts coaching soccer. He is married to an awesome wife and has two great sons who are budding engineers.